CALLED TO LEAD

DR. STEPHEN ADEI

FOCUS ON THE FAMILY

Called To Lead

A Focus on the Family book published by Focus on the Family International.

For international rights and sales inquiries, contact Focus on the Family International: (719) 268-4866, fax (719) 531-3383, email: Intlresources@family.org, or write to Focus on the Family, Attn: International Communications Group 8605 Explorer Drive, Colorado Springs, CO 80920 U.S.A.

LIBRARY OF CONGRESS CATALOGING-IN-PUBLICATION DATA
Adei, Dr. Stephen.
    Called to Lead/Dr. Stephen Adei—
        1st ed. p.   cm.
    Included Bibliographical references
    ISBN 1-58997-274-0

Editor: Tom Neven
Design: Cover, Charles Brock; Interior, Robin Black
        The DesignWorks Group, Sisters, OR

Printed in the United States of America.

CONTENTS

FOREWORD

There is no school for being a husband and a father. As a result, many homes become experimental laboratories, often with disastrous consequences for family members. Some of the products of these failed experiments go on to become the perpetrators of other unsuccessful attempts. This cycle must be broken.

In 10 concise chapters, Professor Adei gives you a recipe for becoming an effective husband and father. Drawing from a rich and wide personal experience, he takes you through the process of leading yourself first and then leading your wife and the rest of the family. As with all institutions, you will discover that the home works best if certain principles are followed. You cannot read through this book and continue to manage your home in a haphazard manner.

This book is based on the biblical principle that the husband and father is the head of the household. Professor Adei explains why the man's leadership role is a responsibility and not merely a position. He calls the man the managing partner of a two-member firm. It is quite obvious that if the leader does a good job, the whole

firm becomes a success. Therefore, if you are serious about making
your family a success, I encourage you to read on.

Kirabo Lukwago
Executive Director
Family Enrichment Ministries
Nairobi, Kenya

ENDORSEMENTS

I wish I had read this book when I was a young man starting out in my ministry and marriage 40 years ago.

REV. DENIS WHITE, FORMER SENIOR PASTOR,
NAIROBI PENTECOSTAL CHURCH

This book ably touches on the key areas that make successful leadership. I would recommend it to all men who are serious about making a success of their God-given responsibility in the home.

PROF. LAZARUS SERUYANGE, PRINCIPAL,
NAIROBI INTERNATIONAL SCHOOL OF THEOLOGY

CHAPTER ONE

THE CHALLENGE OF EFFECTIVE MALE LEADERSHIP

In August 2002, 63 men gathered for three cold days in beautiful Naro Muro in Kenya to discuss male leadership. It was cold in two ways: First, the organiser asked us to leave our wives behind. Second, it was winterly. Although we were close to the equator, the weather was frosty cold because of the altitude. Nevertheless, the experience was worth the effort. I was the nervous and skeptical conference speaker on the topic, "Effective Male Leadership." At the end of the retreat, however, all my skepticism about the uniqueness of male leadership was gone. For one, the Lord taught us all (speaker and participants alike) the unique calling of men as leaders. I never saw a group of men as determined to make a difference in their lives and in the lives of their spouses, families, and co-workers as I saw at the end of the three days. And they were mostly middle- to top-level executives, accomplished men in their professions.

Come to think about it, I was simply "slow of learning." As far back as 1980, at a Bible study in Australia, I found out that when the Bible calls the husband the head of his wife, it refers to male leadership. Men are called to leadership roles in the home and in society. In practice, some abandon the ship and leave home unceremoniously; others, almost one in two, through divorce; and the majority of the rest struggle with their leadership role. It was therefore a unique opportunity for the 63 of us to think through the joys, failures, and challenges of effective male leadership as men. We experienced what members of Promise Keepers already learned:

Promise Keepers discovered, inadvertently, a unique male tendency that God has always understood. Men are more open to His presence and seeking growth in Jesus Christ when they are with other men. There is something about an all-male environment that sets men free to humble themselves under the hand of God and to get to the root of their sin. This is what motivates Promise Keepers to gather men together to pursue integrity, unity of purpose, accountability, honesty, unity and leadership. [1]

Even more interesting was what happened when I had to stay a week longer in Nairobi to give lectures on personal finances and family life. That gave me the opportunity to interact with some of the wives of those men. How did I know they were wives of "Naro Muro Male Leadership Graduates"? The women volunteered to tell me: "We don't care what you did to our men. Whatever it was, it is good for us, and we thank you." In other words, when male leaders are effective, their wives are grateful. Not bad at all! It did not come as a surprise, therefore, when I was asked to write a book on effective male leadership. Even though I had to grapple with the adjective *effective,* for the sake of those grateful wives, I submitted myself to give it a try. It is to those wives of effective leaders of Kenya that I dedicate this book.

TEN REASONS TO FOCUS ON MALE LEADERSHIP

I am now emboldened enough to share some of what transpired at the Naro Muro weekend retreat. But first, let's look at 10 reasons for building effective male leaders.

- *Formal leadership today is predominantly male.* For better or worse, leaders to date have been mostly male. Therefore, effective male leadership may be the single most important determinant of the progress of homes, communities, organisations, and nations—at least in the foreseeable future. Call it male chauvinism, but the reality is that in the formal political, business, and communal leadership arenas, fewer than 10 percent of the leaders are women, Scandinavia excepted.

- *Most male leaders have had leadership thrust on them in the home and society without adequate preparation.* Few enter male leadership with much formal training, and often the training that is provided assumes leadership is gender neutral. Men need a resource that addresses their unique leadership challenges.

FOR BETTER OR WORSE, LEADERS TO DATE HAVE BEEN MOSTLY MALE. THEREFORE, EFFECTIVE MALE LEADERSHIP MAY BE THE SINGLE MOST IMPORTANT DETERMINANT OF THE PROGRESS OF HOMES, COMMUNITIES, ORGANISATIONS, AND NATIONS.

- *In the absence of many real-life mentors, a book on male leadership is a halfway house.* We live in a world of vanishing models and mentors to train the next generation of leaders. As society abandons absolute morality, as many families break up and female-headed households increase, formal training, though not a substitute for mentor-leaders, is required. We need to multiply mentors.

- *Fatherlessness.* A lack of fathers in the home and ineffective male leadership have reached alarming proportions. Yet the role of men as husbands and fathers is irreplaceable. Although husbands and wives are equal, they are different and have complementary roles, all of which need strengthening.

- *A new view of the cries of women.* Many of the cries of women, disguised as a striving for gender equality, can be tied to ineffective male leadership. When men are effective leaders, it brings joy and relief to harassed and oppressed women who are forced to pick up the pieces of failed male leadership.

- *Good leadership is an art to be learned.* The right kind of leadership—transformational, servant leadership—does not come easily to men who seem predisposed toward conquest, dominance, or passivity. Their leadership potential therefore, must be awakened, directed, and enhanced.

- *There is no virtue in ignorance.* The experience of men who have been exposed to effective male leadership indicates that many of the abuse of leadership privileges stem from ignorance and incapacity. The antidote to ignorance is knowledge and hence the need to focus on effective male leadership.

- *Effective male leadership is not chauvinistic.* Effective male leadership is not the antithesis of or opposed to female leadership. These days, some men are paralyzed by the fear that any focus on men will be interpreted as male chauvinism. Nothing is further from the truth. Effective male leadership, in fact, will engender corresponding female leadership and vice versa. They complement each other.

- *Multiply the influence of men.* Effective male leadership simultaneously affects homes, communities, workplaces, and nations positively.

- *It is a divine imperative.* The Bible calls men to lead their wives and family (Ephesians 5:22-33) in the context of Christian families. That call is not to a position of dominance but of service in the steps of Jesus.

This book is, therefore, not about leadership in general but male leadership in particular, with special reference to leadership in the home, where charity begins. It is premised on the proposition that leadership is an art to be learned.

THE MALE LEADERSHIP CRISIS OF TODAY

Increasingly, men are abandoning their leadership role as models and instructors in society. To echo the famous African novelist Chinua Achebe in *Things Fall Apart,* it seems things are falling apart, and the center can no longer hold.[2]

Myles Munroe, in *Becoming a Leader,* is right in his assertion that "whenever a nation has a lack of quality, legitimate and just leaders, national deterioration occurs. It is obvious that our nations are painfully in need of such leaders. The church is desperately in need of leaders. Our homes are crying for leadership. Our youth are begging for leaders. God's answer to all our social, moral and economic problems is qualified on our having just and righteous leaders."[3]

Humans seem to want to start with committees, but God begins with a leader. The fortunes of the leader affect his entire household, community, and nation, as the following examples from the Bible illustrate.

When God wanted to create human beings, He could have created millions of people at a time. He chose instead to create Adam and his companion, Eve, and through them produced nations.

Sin and its consequences resulted in all creation being destined for destruction. But God found one man, a leader, in the person of Noah and saved humanity from extinction. Men, however, continued to rebel and pursue their evil course and, at Babel, even sought to build a tower to the heavens. It all seemed a lost cause with confused languages. In His love, God called a man, Abraham, and through his descendants laid the foundations of a new people of God.

THE CHURCH IS DESPERATELY IN NEED OF LEADERS. OUR HOMES ARE CRYING FOR LEADERSHIP. OUR YOUTH ARE BEGGING FOR LEADERS.

It was not too long before the Israelites found themselves in bondage in Egypt for 400 years, after a brief period of princely treatment under the Hebrew prime minister of Egypt, Joseph. All the time, God was preparing a leader: Moses. In a matter of days, the Hebrews were free. But for their disobedience, they would have settled in Canaan in a short time. But they complained and did not believe God's promises, despite what He had just done for them, so they had to wander in the wilderness for 40 years.

Space will not permit us to recount the stories of Joshua and Caleb, and of the judges, prominent among them being Samson, Japheth, Gideon, and Deborah; of the prophets such as Samuel, Nathan, Isaiah, Jeremiah, Ezekiel, and Daniel, who provided spiritual leadership to Israel.

Then there are David, Solomon, Hezekiah, Jehoshaphat, and Josiah, whose reigns saw Israel assume great heights, and the revivalists such as Ezra and Nehemiah—the rebuilders of postexilic Israel. There were leaders who stood in the breach in times of national crisis such as Elijah, Elisha, Queen Esther, and Mordecai. In the New Testament, leaders such as Peter, James, John, and Paul rose to the top as early leaders of the church.

Leaders are the prime movers of society. However, their impact is not always positive. Israel—and for that matter, all nations and empires—suffered reverses as a result of unjust, illegitimate, and dysfunctional leaders. The rise of a pharaoh who did not remember Joseph meant the nation of Israel suffered bitter slavery for centuries. A foolish decision by Rehoboam, Solomon's son, resulted in an irreparable split among, and damage to, the Hebrew people as a nation. Manasseh,

> LEADERS ARE THE PRIME MOVERS OF SOCIETY. HOWEVER, THEIR IMPACT IS NOT ALWAYS POSITIVE. ISRAEL—AND FOR THAT MATTER, ALL NATIONS AND EMPIRES—SUFFERED REVERSES AS A RESULT OF UNJUST, ILLEGITIMATE, AND DYSFUNCTIONAL LEADERS.

Jezebel, and Jeroboam are other biblical examples of those who brought ruin and death to their people through poor leadership.

In modern times, the likes of Adolf Hitler, Pol Pot of Cambodia, Idi Amin of Uganda, and Saddam Hussein of Iraq are the epitome of leadership gone wrong. One may add that while the world has its Jezebels and Athaliahs on the negative side and the Joan of Arcs and Indira Ghandis on the positive side of female leadership, both functional and dysfunctional leaders have been predominantly male. And that leadership is in crisis.

THE COST OF INEFFECTIVE MALE LEADERSHIP

When male leadership is weak, especially in the home, many a wife is then left to pick up the pieces. Symptoms of crisis in male leadership abound.

The phenomenon of fathers not having time to lead their families is reaching alarming proportions. Unlike the past when families worked together on the farm, modern business is organized in such a way that, apart from weekends, fathers leave home soon after daybreak and return in the evening. It is not uncommon for some fathers, including Christian ones, to be away from home for prolonged periods. In many cases, there is little that can be done, and the parents have to go the extra mile on weekends and at other times to make up for the impact this trend has on their role as leaders.

Some fathers have simply walked out of their homes, leaving their families without male leadership. Single parenthood, which was the exception in the past, has become widespread as divorce escalates and the number of unwed mothers skyrockets. The result is that, among some people, female-headed households are as common as male-headed ones.

The presence of a man by itself does not guarantee effective leadership. Preoccupation with other pursuits, including even legitimate ones such as hobbies and ministry, can undermine leadership in the home. These days the challenge of effective male leadership is compounded by confused gender roles. In attempts to correct historic discrimination against women, some have gone to the extreme to deny gender differences and the unique complementary roles of the sexes.

The effect of these trends on society and men in particular is devastating. In practice, some men may huff and puff; they may bully kids and their women folk; they may resort to antisocial behaviour. The truth is that a man who fails to provide effective leadership at home, in the community, in his church, and in the nation is an unhappy man. That's because most men want to lead, to provide guidance and a model for others to follow, If they fail, they are likely to exhibit tendencies that may mask their true condition. That is why men who are ineffective in their leadership are likely to manifest behaviours that are authoritarian, macho, disruptive, and selfish. In others words, the visible signs may hide the inner insecurity, weakness, and fears of many men as they fail to provide effective leadership.

There are several examples of ineffective male leadership in the Bible. One is King Ahab. Instead of leading Israel, administering justice, and modeling godly character, he coveted Naboth's vineyard. When he felt frustrated in not being able to acquire it, he sulked and moaned and abandoned leadership to his evil wife, Jezebel. The result is that he destroyed his kingship and his family (1 Kings 21–22).

Poor male leadership manifests itself in many ways. First, it manifests itself in frustrated women and wives. In the worst-case scenario, men resort to the only thing they have above women—physical strength; that may explain the rise of domestic violence. Second, ineffective male leadership is a fundamental cause of directionless children. The disruptive impact of the baby boomers—I must confess, my generation—may be partly due to the vacuum created in male leadership during and after World War II, a situation that was exacerbated by the liberal and pseudo-scientific teaching of so-called specialists who advocated a laissez-faire approach to raising children. In the end, a breakdown of society itself is what happens when men refuse to lead.

> MEN WHO ARE INEFFECTIVE IN THEIR LEADERSHIP ARE LIKELY TO MANIFEST BEHAVIOURS THAT ARE AUTHORITARIAN, MACHO, DISRUPTIVE, AND SELFISH.

However, so long as tradition (both secular and ecclesiastical) held sway and the roles of the sexes were defined, the impact of ineffective male leadership remained muted. Today, the situation is different. Many women do not suffer ineffective male leadership silently, thus the call for sexual equality. In addition, the cumulative effect of scientific and technological progress, especially since the Industrial Revolution, has been the transformation of work from the physical to the mental. The modern world of work relies less on brute strength than it does on knowledge.

All these have brought new challenges to male leadership in the sense that one cannot rely on traditional roles and privileges as the basis for a claim to leadership. The male leader must do the work of a leader: providing vision, inspiring and empowering followers to achieve common objectives, whether those followers are a wife and children, members of a church, or employees of a company.

> THE MALE LEADER MUST DO THE WORK OF A LEADER: PROVIDING VISION, INSPIRING AND EMPOWERING FOLLOWERS TO ACHIEVE COMMON OBJECTIVES, WHETHER THOSE FOLLOWERS ARE A WIFE AND CHILDREN, MEMBERS OF A CHURCH, OR EMPLOYEES OF A COMPANY.

The biblical leader is first and foremost a servant leader; this is the model Jesus gave us (see John 13:1-17). In that sense, this book is a call to biblical basics. It has to do with recovering biblical male leadership in the home, at work, and in society. It's not a call to leadership based on a "divine right," physical strength, or alleged male superiority. It's a call to be a model, to mentor and minister to one's followers—to be leaders others want to follow because of their positive influence that arises from their character, competence, and care.

OBSTACLES TO EFFECTIVE MALE LEADERSHIP

Achieving effective male leadership is a major challenge. Five reasons come to mind. In the first place, servant leadership, which is the epitome of effective leadership, does not come easily to men. By constitution, men seek to conquer rather than serve. Service, either by nature or social conditioning, seems to come more easily to many women.

A second factor, which men share in common with women, is the sin nature, which manifests itself in the form of selfishness. Self-centredness is a major obstacle to effective leadership. We would ordinarily seek our self-interest rather than minister to our followers. It takes true conversion and the resulting power of the Holy Spirit to bring this characteristic in check. Yet care for our followers and inspiring them is at the core of effective biblical leadership.

Another reason men may find effective leadership difficult is that traditional models of leadership have been predominantly authoritarian, chauvinistic, and macho. A disciplinarian and strong-willed husband, father, and worker was in the past the norm and still is so in many quarters. There is, therefore, the need to repro-gramme one's mind to be in accord with biblical male leadership.

#4

A fourth cause relates to sheer lack of training and education. The men who gathered in Kenya for the male leadership retreat were good, respectable men who loved their wives and children. They had simply not learned the principles of effective male leadership. Yet since they were above-average workers, husbands, and fathers, others looked to them as models, and rightly so. What they needed was knowledge: how to lead themselves, their wives, and co-workers. In their case, it was more of directing them to focus on what it takes to be an effective male leader.

The Bible points out that lack of knowledge is destructive (Hosea 4:6). Until recently, there was a lack of literature on leadership in general. In fact, more than 90 percent of all leadership books have been written during the last 30 years. Of course, earlier leadership models, from Plato's Philosopher King to Machiavelli's Prince, did not bear the title "leader." And almost none of the present books addresses the issue of male leadership uniquely.

#5

Last but not the least, we believe that Satan loves to see the confusion and pain that emanate from ineffective male leadership. He knows the value that men can bring to families, businesses, and societies—and the consequences when men do not assume their God-given roles. Since our focus is on biblical patterns of effective male leadership in the home, it is important not only to draw attention to the negative impact of the Fall, sin, and Satan, but also to emphasize the positive dimensions of spiritual leadership that Christ brings, to which the next chapter is devoted.

QUESTIONS:

1. Why do you think men are more open to the presence of God when they are with other men?

2. Name some reasons why you think we have a crisis of male leadership today.

3. Why do you think many men are reluctant to take up the reins of leadership in the home?

4. Do you think your wife prefers that you be the leader in the home? Why?

CHAPTER TWO

SPIRITUAL LEADERSHIP
IN THE FAMILY

This book is premised on the belief that leadership is an art to be learned and that the fear of God is the beginning of wisdom. Some people are born with characteristics that mark them early as leaders—people with charisma and intelligence. It's even better if they are extroverts. Many of us recall this typical phenomenon: At the beginning of a new school year, especially at the start of a term when all the students are new, the loudmouth easily gets selected as class captain. Invariably, within weeks there is a revolt because he hasn't learned how to be a leader.

An outgoing personality does not define a leader. Despite our differences, all human beings are born with the potential to exercise leadership, that is, influencing those around you for a common purpose. That is true of leadership in general and particularly so with regard to spiritual leadership in the family.

J. Oswald Sanders, in his Christian classic *Spiritual Leadership*, has given the church an excellent summary of spiritual leadership. Drawing from his work, I want to illustrate four lessons on leadership in the home. First, seeking leadership is an honourable ambition (1 Timothy 3:1). The leadership that is honourable, however, is one that is "achieved not by reducing men to one's service but in giving oneself in selfless service to them" (p. 11).[1]

> DESPITE OUR DIFFERENCES, ALL HUMAN BEINGS ARE BORN WITH THE POTENTIAL TO EXERCISE LEADERSHIP,

The great need of the church and the home is the kind of leadership that is authoritative, spiritual, and sacrificial. It is that kind of honourable servant leadership that Jesus taught, lived, and commanded His followers to practice (Mark 10:43-45).

Second, a great difference exists between natural and spiritual leadership. All effective leaders provide a guiding vision, define how to achieve that vision (a strategy, in other words), and mobilize followers. The essence of leadership is influencing others toward the achievement of a common vision. That much is true of all kinds of leadership. But the natural leader is self-confident, human-centred, and ambitious; makes his own decisions; originates his own methods; enjoys commanding others; tends to be motivated by personal consideration; and is independent. On the other hand, the spiritual leader has confidence in God, seeks God's will, is Christ-honouring (or self-effacing, to use Sanders' word), finds and follows God's methods, delights in obeying God, is motivated by love for God and men, and is God-dependent.

Third, spiritual leadership presupposed certain social, moral, marital, personal, domestic, and intellectual qualities, which are summarized in 1 Timothy 3.

Finally, spiritual leadership translates into practical actions such as prayer, effective time management, the habit of reading, delegation of authority, reproduction of other leaders, and deliberately counting the cost and perils of leadership.

It is important to underscore the fact that the family is the cradle of leadership development. J. Robert

BOTH IN THE BIBLE AND IN CONTEMPORARY SOCIETY, GREAT LEADERS IN OTHER AREAS HAVE OFTEN FAILED ABYSMALLY AT HOME.

Clinton, in *The Making of a Leader,* dubbed a leader's early years as the "sovereign foundation."[2] He recognized that the family is where spiritual servant leadership is learned, tested, and most needed.

Both in the Bible and in contemporary society, great leaders in other areas have often failed abysmally at home. Father Abraham, the father of the faithful, struggled in managing his home (Genesis 16). Isaac's ineffective leadership as a father, coupled with the intrigues of his manipulative wife, Rebecca, brought sibling quarrels to new levels so that from Esau and Jacob, hatred and bitterness have dogged the Middle East ever since (Genesis 27–28).

Jacob's favouritism and lack of control over his family resulted in the abuse suffered by Joseph (Genesis 37). Eli's ineffective leadership at home resulted not only in the defeat of Israel's army, but also his own death and that of his two sons, Hophni and Phinehas (1 Samuel 4). Even David, the godly leader of Israel, the man "after God's own heart," proved ineffective as a spiritual leader of his family, with the result that the sword became the means of settling family feuds in his home. The lesson: Being a leader in society or in the church does not necessarily mean you are an effective leader in the home.

I have had the privilege during my three and a half decades of national and international public service career of working in several countries, including Australia, Britain, the United States, South Africa, Namibia, Ethiopia, and my native Ghana. In most cases, I served under excellent bureaucratic and political leaders. When it comes to the home front, however, some of these leaders have been what I call "successful failures"—the appearance of success hides the realities of moral failure and broken homes. Leadership in the home cannot be assumed to be effective because one is a leader in other realms of life.

That may be the reason why the apostle Paul, in 1 Timothy 3:1-7, portrays domestic life as the test of spiritual leadership:

Here is a trustworthy saying: If anyone sets his heart on being an overseer, he desires a noble task. Now the overseer must be above reproach, the husband of but one wife, temperate, self-controlled, respectable, hospitable, able to teach, not given to drunkenness, not violent but gentle, not quarrelsome, not a lover of money. He must manage his own family well and see that his children obey him with proper respect. (If anyone does not know how to manage his own family, how can he take care of God's church?) He must not be a recent convert, or he may become conceited and fall under the same judgment as the devil. He must also have a good reputation with outsiders, so that he will not fall into disgrace and into the devil's trap.

Paul's summary of the qualifications of spiritual leaders highlights three things:

1) CHRISTIAN MATURITY. The leader "must not be a recent convert" (v. 6). This is important. It is at the core of Christian leadership. It means the spiritual leader must not only know God through repentance and faith in the resurrected Christ, but more than that, he must have a track record of consistent Christian living so that the fruit of the spirit can be observed in him—love, joy, peace, patience, kindness, goodness, faithfulness, gentleness, and self-control (Galatians 5:22-23). Also, it enables the development of one's capacity as a leader and mentor "able to teach" others. The ability to communicate effectively and instruct others is invaluable in the family context,

where fathers are required to instruct their children in the Lord (Ephesians 6:4).

2) **PERSONAL STANDING IN THE COMMUNITY.** Spiritual leadership demands a lifestyle that others would desire to emulate and follow. Paul includes in that lifestyle being above reproach, temperate, self-controlled, not given to drunkenness, not violent but gentle, not quarrelsome, not a lover of money, and not conceited. A man who exercises these qualities will be held in high regard at home and in the community.

3) **DIRECT FAMILY QUALIFICATIONS.** In bygone days when society was predominantly agrarian, leadership was to be learned, tested, and practiced at home. Even then, Paul does not leave that to be inferred but rather identifies explicitly key family qualifications of a spiritual leader. First, the spiritual leader is to be "the husband of but one wife." God's ideal of a leader is a faithful husband, married to one woman monogamously till death. Still on the domestic front, the leader must "manage his own family well and see that his children obey him with proper respect." I wish the church would take heed to the question "If anyone does

THE SPIRITUAL LEADER MUST NOT ONLY KNOW GOD THROUGH REPENTANCE AND FAITH IN THE RESURRECTED CHRIST, BUT MORE THAN THAT HE MUST HAVE A TRACK RECORD OF CONSISTENT CHRISTIAN LIVING.

not know how to manage his own family, how can he take care of God's church?" in its choice of leaders.

THE THREE MS OF SPIRITUAL LEADERSHIP

Spiritual leadership in the family, like effective leadership in other realms of life, involves three things. The leader is called to be a model, a minister, and a mentor. He is to be a *model* because followers see, a *minister* because others feel, a *mentor* because others hear.

> EVERY LEADER IS A MODEL TO OTHERS WHETHER HE IS AWARE OF IT OR NOT. WHILE THAT IS TRUE IN ALL REALMS OF LIFE, IT IS PARTICULARLY SO IN THE HOME.

1) MODEL. Every leader is a model to others whether he is aware of it or not. While that is true in all realms of life, it is particularly so in the home. I have seen doctors who advise their patients to refrain from smoking and excessive use of alcohol, while they themselves smoke like a chimney and drink like fish. Such behaviour will not do in the home. Husbands and fathers must lead by example. They are called upon to model godliness, integrity, and what they tell their children to do. Their actions will affect generations yet unborn.

Husbands, fathers, and all effective male leaders are called upon to model leadership in three areas in particular:

a) *They are to model the fatherhood of God.* I sometimes wonder why God chose to reveal Himself as Father, because it makes me uncomfortable as a fallible earthly father. Yet at the same time, it is the greatest honour to be called "father." It means my children must see in me something, however shadowy, of the fatherhood of God: His providence; His self-sacrifice, especially in sending His own Son Jesus Christ; His unalloyed and unconditional love; His justice, which is perfectly balanced by His mercy; and, above all, His tender loving care.

> CHRISTIANITY TO THE SPIRITUAL LEADER IS NOT "ONCE UPON A TIME I WAS CONVERTED" BUT A DAILY PRACTICE.

Anytime our wives and children pray, "Our Father, who art in heaven . . ." they are actually in some way saying God is like their father. This means that husbands and fathers must strive to become models on earth while confessing their shortcomings and failures in doing so. Our families are not looking for us to be perfect. They know when we genuinely desire to follow Christ.

b) *They are to model* the ideal *husband for their sons and daughters.* I don't think I am unique among fathers, and therefore, what I am going to say has been heard by virtually all fathers. Every child, especially when he or she cannot distinguish good from evil, aspires to be like a father. Wow! What a responsibility for a child to want to be like you. One day, our daughter Eunice went to a wedding with her mother. She was less than five years old. When she came home, her first remark was "Daddy, I want you to marry me." Her mum saved the day by explaining to her that I am the husband of Mummy and that a father cannot marry his daughter. Convinced by Mum's argument, she said, "Then when I grow up, I will like to marry a man like Daddy." I am not sure that now, as a medical officer at 25, she still wants to marry a man like me. But the fact that I still remember the scene after two decades suggests how her childish expression challenged me to live my life as a husband so that my two daughters will want their husbands to be like me.

Husbands have to model the biblical husband who loves his wife unconditionally; nurtures her; respects her; seeks to know and understand her; provides for her emotional, spiritual, and physical needs; and praises her (Proverbs 31:28-31, 1 Corinthians 7:1-7, Ephesians 5:22-33, and 1 Peter 3:7). In so doing he will not only be nurturing a happy, contented wife, but he also will be training his boys to be effective husbands and fathers and giving his daughters lessons on what to look for in a spouse.

c) They model authentic Christianity. The spiritual leader models Christianity in practice, in personal living, at home, at work, and in society. That much is clear in 1 Timothy 3:1-7. Christianity to the spiritual leader is not "once upon a time I was converted" but a daily practice. That means not living with any known sin; admission and confession of wrongdoing when it occurs; asking for forgiveness and the infilling of God's Spirit; reading and meditating on God's Word day and night (Joshua 1:8); giving priority to Christian fellowship, both in a small group and in a local church; personal involvement in some Christian ministry; supporting kingdom business with one's substance; and doing all work as if serving the Lord. Above all else, the spiritual leader is an under-shepherd of Jesus. As such, the single greatest mark of a model Christian is his submission to Jesus as Lord to be honoured and obeyed.

WHEN IT COMES TO CARING FOR THEIR CHILDREN, SOME FATHERS ARE MORE LIKELY TO STRIVE TO MEET THE PHYSICAL NEEDS TO THE NEGLECT OF EQUALLY NEEDED SPIRITUAL AND SOCIAL GROWTH OF THEIR OFFSPRING.

2) MINISTER. The word *minister* is fast losing its meaning. It simply means servant. To minister is to serve. The spiritual leader is a servant leader. The spiritual family leader is the one who dedicates his life to serving his wife and his children and, with them, others.

Paul told the Corinthian Christians that they have many guardians but few fathers (1 Corinthians 4:15). Your family may not be short of teachers, bosses, and bullies, but most likely they will have only you and possibly a handful of truly God-fearing men who will serve them as fathers. The model Leader par excellence is Jesus, who in John 13 demonstrated servant leadership by washing the disciples' feet. He then said, "Now that you know these things, you will be blessed if you do them" (John 13:17). The leaders Jesus seeks are servant leaders, and our families are to learn of this kind of servant at home from their husbands and fathers.

The irony is that in most homes, the one who is served most is likely to be the husband and father. He gets his clothes washed and ironed for him, his house is cleaned, and sometimes others have to collect his dirty socks and shoes unceremoniously left in the living room, as I am often guilty of. This is the exact opposite of the biblical pattern. Granted, certain things need to be done for him, especially if he has to spend a good deal of time earning a living for the family. But when anyone comes into the home of a spiritual leader, there should not be any doubt about who is the servant of all.

Wives are also called to be servant leaders in the home. But the husband and father is also called upon to minister in distinct ways. First, wives need the understanding and support of their husbands as they go through their unique biological and chemical changes during menstrual periods, pregnancies, and menopause.

Second, oftentimes wives and mothers sacrifice their careers and personal development and comfort to help their husbands and children develop. It is expected of spiritual husbands to go the extra mile to ensure that, at appropriate times, they help their wives to realize their full potential. In my family, both children and Dad are grateful that Mum on her own left her career as a teacher to see the children through school. It is a joy that over the last six years she has been encouraged to pursue a degree in theology and a master's in leadership. After all those days, her professional career is resuming at 55! We are praying that she will agree to go for the Ph.D.

Third, wives must be served by helping them in doing household chores. She serves others, from cooking to doing the laundry. And at appropriate times, the spiritual leader must give her a "holiday" to enjoy a totally chores-free day or weekend. Domestic support helps wives feel loved and honoured.

When it comes to caring for their children, some fathers are more likely to strive to meet the physical needs and pay school fees to the neglect of equally needed spiritual and social growth of their offspring. Invariably, that requires making time to be with them, to express warmth, to be at the sideline during their games, to be at parent-teacher meetings, and to listen to them. In so doing, you earn the right to mentor them.

3) MENTOR. A mentor is an experienced and trusted adviser dedicated to the development of another person, usually younger

and less experienced. A prerequisite of being a mentor is being a model and a willingness to serve the one being mentored. But mentoring is more than being a model. Mentoring requires showing special interest in another, to work with him to realize his full potential. It will suffice to quote J. R. Clinton in this area:

Mentoring is a relational process whereby mentor and mentoree work together to discover and develop the mentoree's latent abilities to provide the mentoree with knowledge and skills as opportunities arise. It entails transfer of resources of wisdom, information, experience, confidence, insight, relationship, status, etc. to a mentoree, at an appropriate time and manner so that it facilitates development and empowerment.[3]

SOME PRACTICAL TIPS ON PRACTISING SPIRITUAL LEADERSHIP AT HOME

One may ask: How do men put into practice the three dimensions of spiritual leadership in the family? In anticipation of subsequent chapters of this book and in no way seeking to be prescriptive, the following are some of the practical ways one may lead his family spiritually:

Recognize your under-shepherd role. The spiritual leader is first and foremost an under-shepherd of Jesus Christ, the Good Shepherd (John 10:11). Recognizing this is the first step in servant leadership. An under-shepherd leads his flock on behalf of and under the tutelage and oversight of the Shepherd. As a model, minister, and mentor, a spiritual leader must seek to follow the Lord daily.

> YOUR FAMILY MUST SEE YOU SUBMIT IN OBEDIENCE TO THE AUTHORITY OF JESUS, MEDITATE ON GOD'S WORD DAY AND NIGHT, PRAY FOR YOURSELF AND YOUR FAMILY, AND SERVE THE LORD.

Your family must see you submit in obedience to the authority of Jesus, meditate on God's Word day and night (Joshua 1:8), pray for yourself and your family as Job did (Job 1:5), and serve the Lord. You cannot expect your family to follow you spiritually if you are not following Jesus. "Follow my example, as I follow the example of Christ," said Paul in 1 Corinthians 11:1.

Clarify your mission and vision as a leader. You must be clear about what God requires you to be as a spiritual leader. You must be clear of your leadership role as a husband and a father and commit yourself to it. This is important, because otherwise your leadership will be determined by the socio-cultural traditions of the society we live in, your family upbringing, and the trends of the age rather than by biblical principles.

Set spiritual goals with and for your family. Men are goal oriented. They tend to perform better when they have set clear goals for themselves. I will give a few personal illustrations. My goals as a husband are to make my wife "the happiest woman in the world" and to support her to realize fully her God-given potential. These are goals I know I will die still pursuing, but they motivate me to be a more caring and loving husband. By the time you read this book, Georgina and I will have celebrated our 30th wedding anniversary. I still have a long way to go to achieving these two top goals.

But I have less lofty, but nevertheless important, goals for my family. My wife is not to be exasperated. I am determined to share everything so we shall become one spiritually, in soul and in body. Other goals emerge along the way. Especially now with grown-up children, Georgina needs time to retool for greater ministry outside the home and be independent should the Lord call me home first. She now even drives in Ghana, the first time she is doing so because she feared the reckless drivers there, and I hope she will love going to the bank to sign cheques, something she loathes.

Before I had children, I prayed that each one would accept Jesus before age 13 and that each of the children, as the Lord enabled us, would complete college. We are almost there at the time of writing. For the kids, I took my cue from Luke 2:52, which I interpreted as an admonition to help each of them to grow spiritually, intellectually, socially, and physically.

Seek faithful and trusted allies. In our spiritual leadership, we have the triune God (Father, Son, and Holy Spirit) as our Helper. The Bible is also our best sourcebook. But in addition to these, God has given other people to help us. To that end, our choices are most important. Where one has the choice, the community you live in, the church you fellowship in, and the schools your children attend will make your spiritual leadership easy or difficult. Be wise and prayerful in making decisions in regard to these or you may end up like Lot, who chose to live in Sodom and Gomorrah and ended up losing almost everything. Lot made a choice of residence solely on the basis of economic potential and wound up losing his property and wife (Genesis 13, 14, 18).

The family altar. Pivotal to leading at home spiritually is what is traditionally called the "family altar." It does not refer to any physical altar but a time of Bible reading and prayer as a family. It is the time when the whole household gathers together to pray, worship, share the Scriptures, and encourage one another.

When our children were young, Georgina and I had two such sessions a day. For the six years we lived in Teaneck, New Jersey, the whole family went to school and work in

New York City. The morning family devotions were held in the car (a moving altar, literally) as we braved the daily traffic. The evening ones were quite brief, not because of the children, but because of Daddy, who has the unique gift of sleeping within 10 minutes of silence after 8 p.m.

The challenge is to make the time of worship an exciting one, especially to the youngest, without it becoming boring for the older ones. In our case, when our youngest was about three years old, he would be the one to rally us around, shouting, "Devotion, devotion!" in the evening. And the magic was not our ingenuity but God's gift to the church in the person of Dr. Kenneth Taylor and others who have written several devotional books that kids love and no adult hates.

> THE CHALLENGE IS TO MAKE THE TIME OF WORSHIP AN EXCITING ONE, ESPECIALLY TO THE YOUNGEST, WITHOUT IT BECOMING BORING FOR THE OLDER ONES.

Leadership in the home is the true test of spirituality. This is because one can easily fool almost anybody with our hypocrisy. Not so our family members. That is why I cannot forget a saying of Dr. John Hunter: "If a man says he is filled with the Holy Spirit, I will ask his wife."[4]

QUESTIONS:

1. Why do you think God appointed the man to be the spiritual leader in the family?

2. Some men are natural leaders outside the home. Do you think that makes them more likely to be a good spiritual leader in the home?

3. What does the author mean when he describes someone as a "successful failure"?

4. Why do you think 1 Timothy 3:1-7 looks on a man's leadership in the home as a primary criterion for leadership in the church?

5. Describe the ideal relationship between a mentor and his mentee.

CHAPTER THREE

PRINCIPLES AND VALUES IN PERSONAL LEADERSHIP

In January 2000, I found myself in the position of head of a tertiary institution as Director-General of Ghana Institute of Management and Public Administration. Naturally, it had a board of directors and other senior colleagues to lead and manage the institute. Oftentimes, however, I found myself in a position where everybody looked to me for direction and guidance. Then it dawned on me that the leader has to first lead himself.

Although God is our ultimate Leader, we still have the responsibility to lead ourselves and others. Thus, we may be compared to an army. The general has overall leadership and gives the broad orders, but lower-ranking commanders still have to exercise leadership and accountability. Occasionally, they may seek guidance from the general, and a wise commander will do so, but on a day-to-day basis, he has to get on with the job and lead his men. The parallel in spiritual leadership is seen clearly in the life of Moses.

He was told to go to Egypt to lead the people of Israel out of their bondage and into Canaan. After overcoming his own resistance to take leadership, he took on the challenge of leadership. It took much convincing of his own people and Pharaoh. The 40 years wandering through the desert and the lessons they present for leadership are amply recorded in the book of Exodus. The point I want to emphasize here is that Moses periodically retired to talk to God and seek fresh direction and encouragement—that is, leading himself in order to be a better leader of others.

> ALTHOUGH GOD IS OUR ULTIMATE LEADER, WE STILL HAVE THE RESPONSIBILITY TO LEAD OURSELVES AND OTHERS.

EXERCISE

Consider your life a type of wheel, with several spokes representing different areas of your life, e.g., spiritual life, family life, and professional life (see Box 3.1). On each spoke, indicate how you would score yourself from zero (at the center) to 10 (for the highest or best you can be) on the rim. For example, if you are 50 percent satisfied with the state of your finances, you will mark the midpoint of the financial-life spoke. If you are 25 percent, it will be

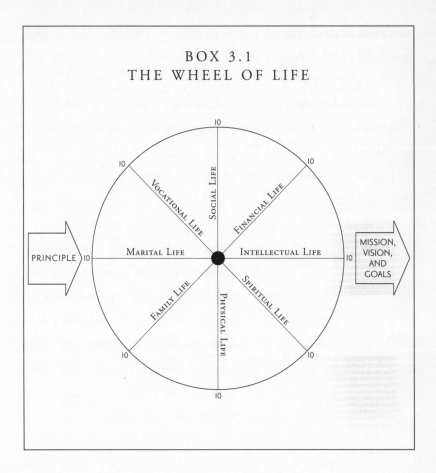

BOX 3.1
THE WHEEL OF LIFE

at one-quarter the distance from the hub. After you have finished all the spokes, connect all the points on the spokes.

How do you interpret the results? The shape of the diagram resulting from connecting the points indicates the balance in your life. The more it resembles a circle, the more balanced your life. On individual spokes, the marks closer to the hub indicate areas you need to give greater attention. But on the whole, your goal should be to work toward getting to the rim in all areas of your life.

Self-leadership is not in opposition to God-dependence. Effective self-leadership will determine whether others will follow you and keep following. Much of what we have to say in this chapter may be summarized in terms of the size, balance, and, above all, the direction of the wheel of life.

MANY HAVE DEVOTED
THEIR LIVES TO
THE PURSUIT OF MONEY,
POWER, AND FAME
TO THE NEGLECT OF
THEIR FAMILY, AND EVEN
ETERNAL LIFE.

The most important part of the wheel exercise is not to condemn oneself but to prompt a positive response. First, where one scored lowest indicates the area that requires the most urgent action to achieve relative balance in one's life. Second, the wheel itself can grow bigger—that is, life's potential is not constrained by a fixed metal rim. Third, the wheel should be driven by your values and principles. Fourth, a wheel is of no use if it does not move. Your mission, vision, and goals—in short, the strategic framework of your life—should give purpose and direction to your self-leadership. Finally, all these must be done in real time, hence the importance of effective time management. In that regard, there is no better place to begin than with the principles of self-leadership.

PRINCIPLES OF SELF-LEADERSHIP

Bookshops abound with books on how to fix life's challenges—money, health, time management, sex life. However, what is lacking in most such books is moral values, with the result that those who follow their quick fixes often end up in worse situations. Thus, before we address the three major elements in leading oneself, namely, personal, strategic planning; self-management; and effective time management, I need to emphasize the key principles that should drive effective self-leadership and management for Christians.

We often hear the expression "climbing the corporate ladder." The question is: Which wall is the ladder leaning against? We do not want to reach the top only to find that we have climbed the wrong wall. Many have devoted their lives to the pursuit of money, power, and fame to the neglect of their family, and even eternal life. We will therefore look at eight guiding principles that should undergird the pursuit of effective personal leadership. These are: organizing principle, values, priorities, capacity building, habit formation, discipline, attitude, and passion.

ORGANIZING PRINCIPLE: Life is made up of a series of choices, because no man can do everything (see Box 3.2, page 50). Thus, at each turn, we have to make choices. Some of the choices can be life-changing, such as the choice of a spouse, career, or place of residence. Others are simple, such as which restaurant to eat at or which clothes to put on for the next function. Most of our day-to-day decisions are made almost unconsciously because they flow from and are guided by our principles, which shape our lives. For example, the businessman is greatly impacted by the bottom line, which is money, while power motivates many politicians in all their relationships.

In their book *First Things First,* Stephen Covey, A. R. Merrill, and R. R. Merrill introduce a powerful concept of the "True North" in personal organization.[1] They use the clock to illustrate our commitments, appointments, schedules, goals, and activities—what we do and how we manage our time. On the other hand, they also use the compass to represent our vision, values, principles, mission, conscience, and direction. They note that many people struggle in life because there is a gap between what they spend their lives on (their clock) as against what they value most (their compass). The authors suggest that people must use their self-awareness, conscience, independent will, and creative imagination, and employ these to find their "True North," or guiding principle in life. While I disagree with their humanistic means of finding direction (because relying on self-awareness, conscience, independent will, and imagination will lead to frustration and not the life Jesus promises), the concept

CHRISTIANS HAVE A "MAGNETIC NORTH," OR A FIXED REFERENCE POINT, IN ALL MATTERS OF LIFE AND CONDUCT. THAT REFERENCE POINT IS JESUS CHRIST, TO WHOM LIFE'S COMPASS SHOULD BE ALIGNED.

of the "compass" and the "True North" are powerful tools to explain what we mean by our organizing principle.

Christians have a "Magnetic North," or a fixed reference point, in all matters of life and conduct. That reference point is Jesus Christ, to whom life's compass should be aligned. The writer of Hebrews states, "Let us fix our eyes on Jesus, the author and perfecter of our faith" (Hebrews 12:2). Our lives must be fixed on an unchangeable reference point, and Jesus meets that criterion in three ways. First, He is the perfect Model and Servant Leader. In His standards we have a rule of leadership. But more important, the reason the clock moves in circles and does not lead anywhere, as a compass does, is because it lacks the sense of pointing to a Magnetic North. Through Jesus' death and resurrection, those who repent of their sins and trust in Him as Saviour have the Holy Spirit in them. They, therefore, become linked to Christ the same way as the compass automatically points toward Magnetic North. Last, but not the least, Jesus has trodden the path He calls His servants to tread, leaving us signposts to follow (John 13:15, 1 Peter 2:21-24).

As a Christian I am called upon to live in accordance with the Word of God; to love my wife, family, and neighbours; and to work hard. How do I balance these and other demands?

Everyone has an organizing principle, which may be overt or implicit. The politician may have a quest for power as his guide, while business people have money, artists fame, and athletes medals. These guiding principles and goals may control their subjects unconsciously. For the Christian, Jesus Christ is the effective organizing principle, his "Magnetic True North." If I am willing to obey Jesus and His Word, I will automatically love my family and neighbour; I will be a reliable, hardworking professional. More than that, my organizing principle will not only see me through the changing scenes of life but into eternity. In a way, being a Christian is to live a highly simplified life. The complication comes only because we are disobedient, fear persecution, and, like our first parents, choose to be self-dependent rather than God-dependent.

VALUES: An organizing principle is indispensable to principle-centred leadership. However, that has to be translated into values. In other words, what does being a servant of Jesus mean in daily living? For example, a major biblical value is personal integrity. This has to do with one's ethics (the theory or belief side) and one's morality (the practice side). A person of integrity exhibits both high ethics and morality in his life. One's ethics can be faulty, however, depending on how his conscience has been educated. One can be a person of integrity, that is, be true to his ethics, and be totally immoral. There are people who believe that there is nothing wrong with sex outside marriage, or that if you kill someone who does not subscribe

> THE EFFECTIVE MALE LEADER IS THE ONE WHO NOT ONLY HAS HIS ORGANIZING PRINCIPLE RIGHT, BUT ALSO HAS TRANSLATED THAT INTO VALUES AND CORE STANDARDS OF BEHAVIOUR.

to your religious beliefs, you are justified; should you die in the act of trying to do so, you are doubly blessed. Faithfully discharging that belief is a mark of integrity, but not the kind of integrity we are discussing here.

For Christians, our ethics matter. The Christian derives his values and principles from the Bible, with Jesus Christ as the Model. Our ethical standards are encoded in the Jesus' Sermon on the Mount, and His leadership is set within the parameters of a Servant Leader.

The effective male leader is the one who not only has his organizing principle right, but also has translated that into values and core standards of behaviour, displaying love, honesty, trustworthiness, integrity, humility, and commitment.

PRIORITIES: A true leader leads himself and leads others. Everyone lives under the constraint of available resources, time, money, logistics, and energy, and these will always be in short supply. A major determinant of leadership is therefore the ability to set priorities to focus on the important. The first step in that direction is to determine what the leader should and should not do and what he should encourage others to take up.

The leader must know that he cannot do everything. In fact, most leaders say no to many pursuits in order to do a few things well. That requires two things. First is the ability to discriminate between what is essential, and what is important but not essential; and between what is helpful but not necessary, and what is trivial. In other words, from the multitude of choices that we face on a

BOX 3.2
PRIORITIES EXERCISE

Write down everything you did in one day (any day will do). If you are thorough and honest, your list could be more than 100 things on a typical day. Now go back and rank your activities according to the following scale, which was developed by Richard Foster:

1. Essential
2. Important but not essential
3. Helpful but not necessary
4. Trivial

How many activities did you list?
How many were Essential and Trivial?
What do they tell you about your use of time?
What do you have to do to reorder your priorities?

Source: Bickel and Jantsz (1998).

daily basis, leaders have to impose on themselves strict rules to determine what must engage them and what they must allow others to do.

In a paper I presented at a training of parliamentary staff in Ghana and Nigeria in March 2003, I shared a priority exercise, presented in Box 3.2. This simple exercise helps to distinguish the woods from the forest.[2]

Leaders do not leave important things undone; rather, they motivate others to do them. They are leaders by virtue of their followers. Leaders, therefore, inspire, motivate, and mobilize others to undertake other functions that they cannot perform themselves. Thus, a complement to prioritizing what should engage the attention, time, and energy of the leader is effective delegation, an art every leader must learn.

The essence of delegation is not to pass on jobs simply because they are unpleasant. Effective delegation is different. It involves the analysis of work to be done to separate it into: (a) what the leader must do himself. For example, "encouraging the heart"—inspiration, motivation, and empowerment of staff, spouse, children. These cannot be delegated. The leader must make time for them. Similarly, vision casting and goal setting may be shared with others, but no leader can delegate them and still be effective. (b) Then there are certain jobs that must be done by the leader with the help of others, or by others with the help of the leader. Managing staff for the CEO is an example of the former while your child's homework is an example of the latter. That is what teamwork is about—two or more people working together to achieve a mutually determined goal. (c) Finally, there is work that the leader must allow other people to do entirely by themselves. Delegation is an exercise in setting priorities for the leader and empowerment for the followers.

Covey excellently captures the setting of priorities in *First Things First* when he distinguishes between the urgent and the important.[3] Many things come to us as urgent matters demanding our attention. Some of these are unimportant. These include some meetings, phone calls, and correspondence. Others, such as crises, deadline-driven problems, and projects are urgent and important. However, many of the so-called urgent and important things arise because weightier matters such as preparation, prevention, values clarification, planning, and training have not received adequate attention in the past. The effective leader focuses on these matters even if they do not appear urgent at the time.

CAPACITY BUILDING: The author of Ecclesiastes has given us an apt statement that sums up what we intend to discuss under capacity building: "If the ax is dull and its edge unsharpened, more strength is needed" (Ecclesiastes 10:10). Leadership ability has to be developed; technical expertise, specific to the job, has to be acquired; and peak performance skills, ranging from information and communication technology to time management, have to be learned. Many fail to become leaders or fail as leaders because of insufficient capacity. That is why effective leaders are perpetual students, always sharpening their ax. In so doing, one sharpens the sword of effective leadership, avoids wasting time, and facilitates the achievement of results.

> EFFECTIVE LEADERS ARE PERPETUAL STUDENTS, ALWAYS SHARPENING THEIR AX. IN SO DOING, ONE SHARPENS THE SWORD OF EFFECTIVE LEADERSHIP.

When I tell people that I have studied more during the last four years than any corresponding period in my life because I am a CEO, they do not believe it. The reality is that never in my life have I found myself lacking on so many occasions as I have since assuming leadership roles in my mid-40s. Worse still, as a leader I am expected to know all the answers, and sometimes subordinates feel let down when I have to refer them to others more expert in a given area. There is a great temptation for a leader to assume omniscience, and that must be resisted. Nonetheless, it behooves every leader to continuously study "as one approved, a workman who does not need to be ashamed and who correctly handles the word of truth" (2 Timothy 2:15).

Capacity building comes through formal training, continuous learning, and practice. True leaders are perpetual learners of the Word of God. They learn from both mentors and mentorees, and through sensitivity to their environment coupled with eagerness to learn from any and all situations. That makes servant leadership an exercise in humility. It pays to continuously enlarge one's capacity as a leader.

HABIT FORMATION: In our book *The Challenge of Parenting: Principles and Practice of Raising Children,* my wife, Georgina, and I emphasized the importance of habit formation in child training. What we said about children is true of all people, especially leaders. We do many things out of habit, including even eating and driving. The trouble is that bad habits are easily acquired and difficult to shed, while good habits are difficult to acquire and easily lost. Others may argue that you cannot teach an old dog new tricks. Fortunately, people are not dogs. Human beings, given the will and the opportunity, are the most adaptable creatures in the world.

Effective Christian leaders identify good leadership habits and learn them. These include the habit of waiting on God in prayer and personal Bible study, the habit of reading good literature, the habit of active listening, and the habit of strategic or systemic thinking, which is the art of thinking in wholes and discerning connections between issues.

BAD HABITS ARE EASILY ACQUIRED AND DIFFICULT TO SHED, WHILE GOOD HABITS ARE DIFFICULT TO ACQUIRE AND EASILY LOST.

There is one habit I learned when I became a Christian in my late teens. That is the habit of waking around 5 a.m. to read the Bible and pray. Now as a CEO and leader, I find that my time between eight a.m. and five p.m. is not my own. But the habit of waking up early these days, sometimes by four a.m., enables me to spend time alone with God, organize my activities, write papers and books, and still spend about an hour quality time with my wife almost each morning we are together.

Good habits can be learned anytime. I had a bad habit of spending everything I earned plus more, which resulted in debt. That habit was the result of an overreaction to someone's comment that as an aspiring economist, I would be stingy in life. Thus, I became irresponsibly overgenerous, sometimes borrowing on plastic cards to help others, some of whom simply took advantage of me. I was about 46 years old, indebted, and faced with financial ruin if I lost my job when I decided to practice the "pay God, pay yourself, and pay your bills" principle found in my book *12 Keys to Financial Success*. This simply means that you should dedicate a minimum of 10 percent of your earnings to the kingdom of God, set aside a further 10 percent to save and invest, and live within 80 percent of your income. Following that principle, I was debt-free in six years and financially independent, which means I can sustain my desired lifestyle in Ghana if I am no longer earning a regular income. Come to think of it, there also are well-tested habits of wealth creation, having a good marriage, raising godly kids, and cultivating righteous living. But equally important are practical habits that are so essential for managing oneself—taking care of one's health through right eating habits, exercise, stress management, and regular medical checkups.

DISCIPLINE: Habits come by discipline. Mental, moral, and physical discipline is the bedrock of habit formation and the striving for excellence. Self-discipline is a hallmark of an effective leader.

The leader, by definition, leads others. Often the buck stops with him as a father, supervisor, or CEO. Many leaders are responsible for disciplining others. But who disciplines the leader? He must discipline himself. Failure to do so will lead to what has happened to many leaders, from President Richard Nixon to managerial leaders of Enron Corporation: the "successful failure syndrome."

When it comes to discipline, two people in the Bible are my models: Joseph and Daniel. Joseph is a model when it comes to moral discipline. Many would chase the opportunity to flirt with a woman of influence and authority. But at the peril of his life, and definitely of false imprisonment, Joseph refused to go to bed with his master's wife because he feared God (Genesis 39). Daniel and his three friends in the book that bears his name showed discipline in their diet, in their studies, and in their work as public servants. Their discipline, coupled with the fear of God, led them into a fiery furnace and the lions' den. The same discipline also took them to the top of their careers, and they earned the respect of kings and God's people for eternity.

> HABITS COME BY DISCIPLINE. MENTAL, MORAL, AND PHYSICAL DISCIPLINE IS THE BEDROCK OF HABIT FORMATION AND THE STRIVING FOR EXCELLENCE.

These days, *discipline* seems a dirty word. People want instant drug-induced slim bodies, instant coffee, instant wealth. Talk about self-control and self-discipline and you sound like somebody from Mars. Yet it pays to bring yourself under control and to follow self-imposed regulation with respect to time, money, eating, and mind to achieve greater things for God, country, family, and yourself. We must redeem discipline from its modern neglect.

ATTITUDE: It is said that attitude accounts for 85 percent of human achievements while skills account for 15 percent. While we are not in a position to vouch for the mathematical precision of the weights, there is no doubt that leadership is a matter of attitude.

To be a leader, one must be willing to take responsibility, not only for oneself, but for others as well. Stephen Covey lists "The 7 Habits of Highly Effective People" as follows: "Being proactive," "Beginning with the end in mind," "Putting first things first," "Thinking win-win-win," "Seeking first to understand, then to be understood," "Synergy," and "Sharpening the saw."[4] And he calls them habits. They may as well be called disciplines. However, the most important point is that underlying the "seven habits" are two important attitudes. One is an attitude of abundance, the view that there is room for all. The second, which we have already alluded to, is personal discipline.

People who accept responsibility, people who have a spirit of abundance and generosity and who go out of their way to serve others and solve big problems for the common good, are followed by others. A person with followers—willing followers, I mean— is a leader.

People aspire to leadership for different reasons. Some do so to be popular. Others do so to have authority to order others about. Others seek leadership to amass wealth, especially in many Third World countries. The servant leader must seek leadership to serve. A servant attitude is what Jesus requires of His under-shepherds.

Some Christians, however, have avoided leadership or, more specifically, not contested for leadership in public life because they think doing so will mean they are not humble. The result is that oftentimes, evil men and women are left to govern. Humility must be our attitude, but it has to do with the heart and our motivation. If our heart is right with God, then the Bible says seeking leadership is a noble pursuit (Romans 2:8; 1 Timothy 3:1).

PASSION: I wish I could jump over this word *passion*; it has become so associated with the hedonist's view of unbridled sinful quest for pleasure—sexual and material pleasure—that to mention it as a major leadership quality risks condemnation. But it is worth the risk, because a leader who is not excited, enthusiastic, and committed to a mission and vision will attract no followers.

> JESUS WAS PASSIONATE ABOUT HIS MISSION, WHICH WAS TO DO HIS FATHER'S WILL, EVEN TO THE POINT OF DEATH ON THE CROSS.

Jesus was passionate about His mission, which was to do His Father's will, even to the point of death on the cross. All great leaders of history had a passion for their cause. And that was true of those who fought for and passed on the true faith in Jesus to us—Paul, Athanasius, Luther, Wesley, Moody, and Billy Graham, to mention a few.

I once heard the Rev. John Stott, pastor emeritus of All Souls Church in London, talk about an African-American preacher. In preparing his preaching, Stott said this man "reads himself full, prays himself hot, and lets himself go." That is passion. The "lets himself go" refers to his passion to preach the gospel under the anointing of the Holy Spirit.

By passion, we are not necessarily referring to exhilarating, charismatic exuberance. Not all people are extroverts. And charisma may give one a head start in leadership, but it's never a sufficient condition for effective leadership. Rather, we are referring to conviction, a firm belief and commitment to one's goals, which, for the effective Christian male leader, should include:

- Love for Jesus
- A commitment to wife and family
- Specific vocational leadership goals

Effective leadership begins with the inner strength of a person, and that is defined by his principles. These have been discussed under the leader's "organizing principle," or what he aligns his life to, his values, his life's priorities, his capacity, his habits, his self-discipline, his attitude toward responsibility, and his passion to lead. The importance of these is that they define the quality of leadership.

In the next two chapters we move from the principle of self-leadership to the practice of leading oneself.

QUESTIONS:

1. Compare Moses' leadership challenge with one you might have faced.

2. What is missing from most books on leadership? Why do you think that is the case?

3. What is meant by "principle-centred" leadership?

4. What is a major determinant of leadership abilities?

CHAPTER FOUR

STRATEGIC SELF-LEADERSHIP AND MANAGEMENT

We have now come to the point where we must address the practical aspects of leading oneself. This has to do with strategic personal leadership and self-management to put each room in the house of your life in order, so to speak, as well as effective time management to reflect and implement one's life strategies and self-management goals.

Two things have necessitated most of the preceding chapter. The first is the unfamiliarity with the concept of self-leadership. The second is the fact that those who hit the trail with how-to books often forget that principles must precede precepts. Having addressed these two phenomena, we are in a position to look at three key elements in the practice of self-leadership, namely:

- Working out a strategic framework for one's life
- Managing the various departments of one's life
- Effective time management

We will cover the first two in the rest of this chapter and take up the third in the next chapter.

A STRATEGIC FRAMEWORK FOR PERSONAL LIVING

Students of management, especially at the graduate school level, are familiar with the concept of strategic management, which is now part of almost all MBA programmes. But even if you have not been to business school, you will find that the key concepts and their application to effective living are very simple. The business world was the first to recognize that the most important ingredient in success at the corporate level is the direction given by its leadership. Strategic management in business involves a definition of a company's mission, its medium- to long-term objectives,

LONG BEFORE MODERN BUSINESS SCHOOLS, THE BIBLE HAD IDENTIFIED THAT WITHOUT VISION, A PEOPLE PERISH (PROVERBS 29:18).

broad strategies to achieve the objectives, and managing the change required to attain the vision. In doing so, much effort is expended in examining the company or institution's economic, social, political, technological, and ecological environment to identify a niche and its competitive advantage. In order to achieve this, strategic managers study the strengths, weaknesses, opportunities, and threats of and toward the establishment. Once a course of action is determined, the strategy is implemented, either by continuously planned adjustments or through major transformation and restructuring, which is sometimes called reengineering of the company.

Long before modern business schools, the Bible had identified that without vision, a people perish (Proverbs 29:18). It is known that people who are mission- and vision-driven tend to achieve at least twice what their counterparts accomplish in life. Jesus, in advising His followers to plan ahead, said that anyone going to battle or building a house must first find out whether he has the resources to complete the task (Luke 14:28-30). Jesus was actually advocating for strategic planning. The lesson in the story of the rich fool in the Bible was not that working hard and making provision for the future are bad. At the core of his folly was that in all his planning, he behaved as if man was immortal and independent of God (Luke12:16-21).

In order to give a spark to our lives and to provide leadership to others, we need a strategic framework for personal living. To be effective, a leader must explicitly and strategically manage his life. The application of the core elements of strategic thinking and management to one's personal life is self-leadership.

There are eight factors in providing a strategic framework for personal living, namely: a personal mission statement, vision, roles, values, goals, a personal strategic plan, an implementation plan, and commitment and discipline to implement the plan through monitoring and evaluation. The good news is that, given the right attitude, everyone can handle all that these entail. There is no need for a college diploma to lead oneself.

A Personal Mission Statement

A personal mission statement is the *raison d'être* of one's existence—the purpose for one's living. In a personal mission statement, you are stating clearly to yourself the very reason for your existence. In a class I teach called "Balancing the Personal, Relational, and Public Life," I challenge people to go about making personal mission statements by seeking to answer questions such as:

- What would I like to be remembered for when I die?

- Why am I on earth?

- What do I value most in life?

- If I had all the necessary resources and capacity, what would I like to do?

- What are the significant roles I play in my life?

- What inspires me most?

A true mission statement will be such that, if you lived by it, your basic needs (e.g., physical, intellectual, spiritual, social, and financial) and God-given aspirations would be met without compromising deeply held values. Moreover, a mission statement must integrate all the key roles of a person, such as father, husband, worker, and leader in the church. A mission statement that creates imbalance in one's life is not worth anything.

I normally do not ask people to aim at achieving a perfect personal mission statement, if ever there was one. Nor do I, for that matter, initially seek to clearly distinguish between mission, vision, and goals, provided that in the end you arrive at a purposeful view of the future that is strong enough to propel you to action.

> A MISSION STATEMENT THAT CREATES IMBALANCE IN ONE'S LIFE IS NOT WORTH ANYTHING.

Examples of personal mission statements are as follows:

1. "To be a person whom my God, wife, children, and colleagues can be proud of."

2. "I want to be known by my family as a caring and loving husband and to display excellence in all the work I do in this life."

3. "To be a billionaire at the age of 45."

4. "To serve Jesus Christ in my generation."

While I may not endorse all of these examples, they do illustrate personal mission statements from people of various walks of life.

Now comes my punch line for Christians: There are parameters within which a Christian draws his or her mission. Are Christians free to determine their own mission on earth? My answer is yes and no. No, because the purpose for which we were created and redeemed is clearly stated in the Bible: "Fear [reverence, respect, live for] God and keep His commandments, for this is the whole duty of man" (Ecclesiastes 12:13). We also read in 1 Peter 2:9, "You are a chosen people, a royal priesthood, a holy nation, a people belonging to God, that you may declare the praises of him who called you out of darkness into his wonderful light."

> CHRISTIANS ARE TO LIVE THEIR LIVES IN A WAY THAT WILL BRING PRAISE AND GLORY TO GOD THEIR MAKER AND JESUS THEIR SAVIOUR.

In other words, Christians are to live their lives in a way that will bring praise and glory to God their Maker and Jesus their Saviour. This is the purpose of their creation and redemption. All their actions and roles must be guided by that purpose.

So a true Christian's ultimate purpose in life is tied to his redemption. However, the individual still has to interpret his calling as a saint in a way that is meaningful to him. For example, while we are called to love the Lord, and to be loving husbands and fathers as well as faithful workers, the mode of meeting these different roles will vary between a pastor and an airline pilot and between a teacher and a labourer. This is where a personal mission statement becomes necessary, useful, and motivating. My mission statement, "To serve Jesus Christ in my generation," while not as innovative as others may be, is meaningful to me as an adaptation of what is said about David in Acts 13:36. It is anchored to obedience to God and service to men.

I want to encourage you to pause and reflect on the purpose of living. Using the space below, draft a personal mission statement that can be used to reply to anyone who asks you the reason or purpose of your life.

My mission in life is:

_____

_____

_____

_____

_____

_____

_____

_____

_____

Vision

Closely linked to mission is a personal vision statement. In fact, if you have a vision that stretches to the end of your life, it may be synonymous with mission statement. I have good reason to distinguish between vision and mission, however. I think that when the Bible says, "Where there is no vision the people perish" (Proverbs 29:18), it refers to both mission and vision. The essence of a vision is to capture a desired future that integrates what one will do and achieve within a given period. Vision, for the majority of us, is best planned to span a period of 10 to 20 years, depending on your age. I recommend to those under 40 to set their vision within a 15- to 20-year horizon, and 10 years for older folks. Let us note here that there is nothing sacrosanct about the time spans. I am only being practical.

THE ESSENCE OF A VISION IS TO CAPTURE A DESIRED FUTURE THAT INTEGRATES WHAT ONE WILL DO AND ACHIEVE WITHIN A GIVEN PERIOD.

I recall envisioning at the age of 46 that within 10 years I would be settled in my native country, Ghana, be financially self-sufficient, be in a position to contribute to the building of my motherland, and possibly be working full time in a Christian ministry. All that was captured in my vision statement. Most of that was achieved in six years. Vision in this practical context translates mission into medium- to long-term framework. Drawing on the world of photography, mission statement is the long shot, vision statement is the medium shot, and goals are equivalent to the close-up shot with specific details.

Dreams and imagination are seeds from which vision emerges. Imagination feeds vision, but vision is more than imagination.

Vision is a picture of the future that catalyses each day's actions toward bringing into reality a dream, a mental picture of what one must and ought to be. In that regard, everyone at one time or the other has the beginnings of a future vision of themselves, though in many cases that vision remains in the dream world and never gets translated into reality.

Vision fuels passion and passion in turn drives vision achievement. I have found that people rarely achieve their personal vision exactly as they set out. Even so, my experience is that vision-driven people tend to achieve twice as much—or more—as those without a vision. People with vision tend to lead focused, contented lives.

Your vision statement must capture simply but concretely what you want to be in 10, 15, 20, or 25 years from now, and that by the grace of God. I encourage you to pause here and answer this question prayerfully: *By God's grace, what do I want to achieve in the next 10 or 15 or 20 years? What kind of person do I want to be?* Your vision statement will look like your mission statement but put in a form you can implement in the specified time frame. If you have difficulty with personal vision statement, read on to the goal setting below. Once you have set your goals for, say, 10 years, you can work backward to the more comprehensive vision statement.

Roles

Your strategic plan for self-leadership must enable you to fulfill the leader's roles as a spouse, parent, worker, community leader, and, most important, as a child of God. In fact, the cause of the "successful failure" syndrome is the failure of many a leader to ensure that he does not overemphasize his public role at the expense of his personal and relational roles. I have found that an excellent way to test your vision is to check whether the realization of the vision would enable you to fulfill your personal leadership roles. In that regard, setting individual goals for each of the key roles is an antidote to imbalance in the life of the leader. (See the wheel of life in Box 3.1, page 43.)

VISION FUELS PASSION AND PASSION IN TURN DRIVES VISION ACHIEVEMENT.

Values

What does being a servant of Jesus mean in daily living? The Christian derives his values from the Bible, with Jesus Christ as the Model. The effective male leader is the one who not only has his organizing principle right, but also has translated that into values and core standards of behaviour, displaying love, honesty, trustworthiness, integrity, humility, and commitment.

Goals

The bridge between mission-vision and action is goals. In my book *Twelve Keys to Financial Success,* I give 10 reasons why goals are important. Goals must, as far as possible, be Specific, Measurable, Attainable, Realistic, and Time-bound (the so-called S.M.A.R.T. goals). In a nutshell, setting clear goals provides signposts on the path to achievement of your vision. Moreover, it is a catalyst for action and enables you to measure progress.

Sometimes I hear some Christians argue as if setting goals and living by faith are opposites. For me, goals constitute a statement of faith in the sense that they are set prayerfully and become an "assurance of things hoped for."

In personal strategic planning, goals are best set for each of the principal areas of life—spiritual, financial, physical, intellectual, marital, parental, social, and vocational. The starting point in goal setting is to make a list of your desires. For example, in the intellectual realm, a desire list may include:

> I would like to have a college diploma.
>
> I wish to keep myself updated on key financial issues.
>
> I want to improve my reading speed.

However, desires are not goals. For them to be goals, they must be S.M.A.R.T. (specific, measurable, attainable, realistic, time-bound). Thus, while the three examples above are desires, the following meet the criteria of goals:

> I will complete my college diploma in four years.
>
> I am subscribing to *The Wall Street Journal* at the end of the month.
>
> Within a year I will double my reading speed.

The following are some practical 10-year goals I set for myself at the age of 46.

General: To be financially independent and resign from the United Nations to return to my home, Ghana.

Spiritual: Sustain personal devotions and, with my wife, read through the Bible every two years.

Parental: To see all three older children through college with the fourth about to enter college.

Intellectual: To complete my master's degree in theology and write 10 books.

Financial: To be debt-free and have savings and investments of $365,000.

Social: To maintain a network of friends and write one letter to each of them (about 100) each year.

Physical: To have a medical checkup yearly, exercise, and monitor my diet.

Professional: To take early retirement from the U.N. and go into ministry.

Marital: To support "Honey" to complete her bachelor's in theology, possibly master's, prepare her for ministry in the "empty nest" years, and ensure her independence should I die first.

What happened? Well, in most of the areas the goals were achieved in six years. Of the rest, God drastically altered one in the professional area. In a couple of areas, and you can guess them (social and physical), there have been some slippages, and I am closing in on my intellectual goals. The most important thing is that goal setting has made life more exciting and most fruitful.

Personal Strategic Plan

Strategies are the means of achieving your goals. Let us use an illustration in the financial realm. If someone desires to be a millionaire at age 60, then starting at age 20, he should invest $157 per month (assuming 10 percent return). The means of achieving his financial targets may be a combination of monthly savings and investments, occasional lump-sum investments, converting nonperforming assets into income-generating instruments, etc. These will be his strategies to achieve the financial goal to be a millionaire.

Similarly, improving one's marriage may require spending additional time together, meeting each other's expressed needs, and reading the Bible and praying together. Strategies must be developed for each goal.

A strategic plan, to the business person, is a document that embodies the mission-vision, goals, strategies, and actions for implementation as well as how they will be monitored and evaluated. I recommend a parallel document in organizing your personal life, albeit in a far simpler form. While today my personal strategic plan is just one page, most people may do with a few pages. It must be action-oriented. An outline of a personal strategic plan may look like this:

Sample Personal Strategic Plan

Mission: To become the leader of my people at the age of 55, being a model in character, competence, and care.

Vision: To be the head of my unit in five years, with family moved from downtown to a suburban area.

Roles: To be:
- a loving husband
- a caring father
- an efficient worker
- a servant of Jesus
- a leader in my community/church

Values: To live by faith in Jesus, expressed in obedience, personal integrity, honesty, and trustworthiness, and in love for my spouse and children.

Goals: (See the 10-year goals on page 72.)

Strategies and Actions:
- Stop buying on credit.
- Place a standing order for bank to invest 10 percent of net income in a mutual fund or unit trust each month.
- Accelerate debt repayment by 25 percent each month.

Monitoring • Review projects every quarter with
and Evaluation: spouse and make modifications as needed.

Implementation Plan

This may take the form of a grid or table that pulls together goals, objectives and targets (targets break goals into finer details), strategies, and the type of attitude, knowledge, habits, sacrifices, and actions that are required to achieve the goals. (See Box 4.1, page 77) The personal strategic plan can be as sketchy or detailed as you wish, provided:

- it sums up your aspirations;

- it is in line with your values;

- prayerfully, you are at peace with it; and

- the plan gives direction and purpose to your life.

The actual form is not the essence. The process is as important as the product. It is meant to give direction to your life.

Mission, vision, values, and roles are placed on top of the grid in Box 4.1 for good reason. They constitute the main coordinates of self-leadership. They are the underlying factors that must give direction to self-management. The grid itself indicates that for each area of life, you need to set goals. The goals are to correspond to the strategic areas listed. Even though one row is given for each area of life, as many rows as necessary can be created under each subsection. In other words, you could have two, three, or four spiritual goals. The number of goals per area of life is not fixed, but more than three goals per sector could be too many, and I would not recommend more than five.

Under "Objectives and targets," goals must be broken down into actionable, measurable indicators of success within one to three or, at most, five years, depending on your management horizon. For starters, I recommend a one-year operational framework. Against the objectives and targets indicate the strategies to be employed to achieve each of the objectives.

Monitoring and Evaluation

. TO KEEP DOING THE SAME THINGS AND EXPECT DIFFERENT RESULTS IS THE HEIGHT OF SELF-DECEPTION.

We now come to the most difficult part of translating strategic plans into reality: the discipline to acquire and implement new habits, new ways of doing things—what it takes to make the dream come true. I have selected five things you must work on to achieve your goals and objectives, namely, attitudes, knowledge, habits, actions, and sacrifices, as indicated in the last column of Box 4.1. To keep doing the same things and expect different results is the height of self-deception. Giving new direction to your life often requires changes in attitude and the acquisition of new skills and new habits. You may have to make sacrifices to achieve goals. This last column is meant to encourage

BOX 4.1
PERSONAL STRATEGIC PLAN
Simple Framework for Self-Management[2]

Mission _____

Vision _____

Values _____

Roles _____

Area	Goals	Objectives and targets	Time Frame	Strategies	Attitudes, knowledge, habits, actions, and sacrifices required
1. Financial					
2. Intellectual					
3. Physical					
4. Marital					
5. Family					
6. Spiritual					
7. Social					
8. Vocational/ Professional					

readers to count the cost involved in realizing their personal strategic plan.

To further assist readers to complete the grid for themselves, I have provided below an illustration of how the row on finances can be completed using a real-life case (with certain details altered for the sake of privacy):

Goal: To achieve financial independence by accumulating $500,000.

Objectives: To save part of salary over the period, which is expected to grow to $500,000.

Time Frame: 10 years.

Strategies: To increase savings and investment from earnings to 20 percent a month over 10 years.

To dispose of second family car, nonperforming assets, and antiques in the attic.

To start a family business out of the hobby of facilitating friends' parties.

Attitudes, knowledge, and habits: Continue monthly savings habit, but at double the current rate of 10 percent. Put in a standing order at the bank next week to deduct investment at source.

Control habit of buying on impulse and using credit cards outside the family budget.

Leading and managing yourself effectively does not come easily; it requires discipline, which many of us do not like. The good news is that as soon as you set out to try it, especially in a family setting, it soon becomes fun and infectious.

The next chapter will provide you with tools for implementing these personal leadership skills on a monthly, weekly, and daily basis.

QUESTIONS:

1. What does it mean to say "principles must precede precepts"?

2. Why is a vision necessary for leadership?

3. What should be included in a personal mission statement?

4. Are there any principles that should guide a Christian's mission statement?

CHAPTER FIVE

MANAGING ONESELF THROUGH EFFECTIVE TIME MANAGEMENT

In an age with instant everything, it may seem odd to talk about time management. Yet all good things require time. It takes time to grow spiritually, because it requires reading the Bible and obeying its teaching, praying, fellowshipping, and serving the Lord. There is no shortcut to Christian maturity. It takes time to build a financial nest. It takes time to acquire marketable skills, which, these days, often include a college education.

At this stage, why not stop to do a little exercise before you become prejudiced by what follows? List five things you value most in your life. Are they your marriage, children, business, money, work, parents, friendship, power, vacation, recreation, or church? Do that before reading the next paragraph, even if you have to do it mentally, though it is better if you write it down.

Now look back over the past week, preferably with your diary next to you. Did these things that matter most to you appear on your calendar? How much time did you devote to the items that are most important to you? How about your different roles as a child, spouse, parent, worker, or church member? Was there a balance in your use of time regarding these roles?

> NO ONE MAKES UP FOR TIME LOST. YESTERDAY IS GONE; TOMORROW IS YET TO COME, AND WE ARE BETTER OFF PLANNING FOR IT.

The tragedy of many leaders is that the proper use of time does not appear on their most-important list. Our vision, goals, and roles must drive our use of time and not vice versa. This is because:

- *Time management is self-management.* What is at stake is not the clock but what we apply our *lifetime* to achieve.

- *Time management is an exercise in choice.* We make choices between the important and the urgent, between our priorities and other imposed demands.

- *Time management is an exercise in discipline.* If you want to check that out, find out how long most people's New Year's resolutions last.

- *Time management involves skills and tools.* These are what you will find in the rest of this chapter.

TEN CHARACTERISTICS OF TIME

Time is probably the single most important resource we have to implement our vision. Knowing some characteristics of time will aid in its management:

- *Time is an asset.* In fact, for most people, it is the most important asset they have in growing spiritually, physically, mentally, socially, and morally.

- *Time is precious.* Not only is time an asset, it is a precious asset.

- *Time is an "equal opportunity" resource.* The Lord has given the rich and the poor, the old and the young, the CEO and the labourer equal time: 365 days a year and 24 hours a day.

- *Time is limited.* The Bible tells us that an average lifespan is up to 70 or 80 years, and despite medical advances it is only a few who go beyond 80 years and enjoy it.

- *Time for all that matters.* Yes, we all have time to do what matters most to us. "I am busy" often means "It is not my priority."

- *Time is a passing opportunity.* No one makes up for time lost. Yesterday is gone; tomorrow is yet to come, and we are better off planning for it. But we have only today to live. Time lost is irredeemable.

- *Not all time is equal.* Oh, that young people would not need to learn this the hard way! There is an opportune time for everything under the sun. For example, some people do not make the best of their lives because they defer skills acquisition to their middle years instead of doing so while younger.

- *Time is linear.* Literally, tomorrow follows today. Most important, life is organized in such a way that there are always certain preparatory periods that act as platforms for future achievements. Few people can skip what needs to be done at one stage of life and still do well in subsequent stages. High school education comes before college education, for example.

- *Time has an eternal dimension.* I believe there is an eternal dimension to time. "Man is destined to die once, and after that to face judgment" (Hebrews 9:27). We shall all stand before God. The eternal dimension of time demands that we live today with eternity in view.

> WE SHALL ALL STAND BEFORE GOD. THE ETERNAL DIMENSION OF TIME DEMANDS THAT WE LIVE TODAY WITH ETERNITY IN VIEW.

- *Time has to be managed.* It stands to be said that if time is a precious asset, is a passing opportunity, and has an eternal dimension, then it must be managed and used effectively.

FOUR PRINCIPLES AND PRACTICES OF EFFECTIVE TIME MANAGEMENT

In Ephesians 5:15-16, the Bible reads, "Be very careful, then, how you live—not as unwise but as wise, making the most of every opportunity, because the days are evil." In our book *Seven Keys to Abundant Living With No Regrets,* we introduced four principles of effective time management:

- *Principle 1:* Commitment to Make a Difference
- *Principle 2:* Redeeming the Time
- *Principle 3:* Making the Most of the Time.
- *Principle 4:* Reckoning with Time

Principle 1: Commitment to Make a Difference

Ephesians 5:15-16 is a call for a deliberate and conscious effort to control the use of one's time for good and to achieve one's goals. The reasons and need for such a commitment are many. Many demands compete for our time. The average worker has about 80 percent of the ordinary day predetermined: 10 hours of going to work, including travel time; two hours devoted to preparing food and eating; eight hours of sleeping time. Up to 20 hours are gone! Thus, there is the need to improve the content of the already allocated time and to make "the most of every opportunity," as you are not going to get more than 24 hours in a day.

In other words, time management must be driven by what is most important to us—our relationship with God, our spouse, and our family. It must be driven by our mission-vision goals. We should commit to giving attention to these on our calendars. Otherwise, we will go down the path of the majority, characterized by unfulfilled dreams.

Cemeteries are filled with unrealized and unfulfilled dreams. This is because many of those buried there succumbed to societal pressures, tradition, and the neglect of their God-given destiny. Subconsciously, our time management is driven by education, promotion at work, money, and keeping up with the Joneses. There is nothing wrong with these, by themselves, but they must be regulated and directed by our life goals.

> TIME MANAGEMENT MUST BE DRIVEN BY WHAT IS MOST IMPORTANT TO US — OUR RELATIONSHIP WITH GOD, OUR SPOUSE, AND OUR FAMILY.

You should aim to do a broad time budget, for the major seasons of life, and translate it into annual, monthly, weekly, and daily schedules. Commit yourself to predetermined values, goals, and vision—subject, of course, to new directions from God. If we don't, our time management will be reduced to a mechanical manipulation of tools such as calendars, which themselves are of little help unless they are guided by our commitment to make the most of our lives.

Principle 2: Redeeming the Time

By redeeming the time, I mean the deliberate attempt to reallocate part of our low-priority time for high-priority purposes. In order to assist you in redeeming the time, I've prepared the following checklist so you can examine your use of time under the following headings.

CAPTURING TWO TO FOUR HOURS A DAY makes the difference. We cannot avoid going to work, eating, and sleeping. This leaves most people only about two to four hours of discretionary time a day. This time must be identified and captured for higher ends. In identifying these hours, the following suggestions may be helpful:

- Examine your 24-hour day to identify your discretionary time. In other words, which part of the 24 hours can I redeem? For example, I have realized that 5 a.m. to 8 a.m. is a period I can set aside for time with God and my wife, and to do quality thinking and reading. I am an early sleeper, so that is easy to do. Others may find 9 p.m. to midnight equally good.

- Use a daily list of "must do things" to avoid being sidetracked. The list should reflect your top three or so priorities—the important items you must attend to each day.

- Learn to say no to some secondary demands. Saying no to some demands to do a few things better is a secret to fruitful living.

- Learn effective delegation, work sharing, and shedding work others can do.

- Carry useful work such as reading material to fill in during unavoidable time wasters, such as plane delays or having to wait for a bus.

- Improve your skills to avoid spending twice the time needed for a task.

- Control "time thieves" such as unnecessary watching of TV, idle conversation, drop-ins at work, and long hours on the Internet.

- Find your most productive time and block it out as your discretionary time.

WEEKLY USE OF TIME. We have seven days a week. Even though God gave six days for us to work, I have no quarrel with modern labour unions extracting a five-working-day week from employers. This is because there is more work to be done within the family and society than what goes on from 8 a.m. to 5 p.m., Monday through Friday. The most important things are the following:

- *Weekends:* Saturday and Sunday constitute almost 30 percent of one's life. That chunk of our time must be redeemed and consciously applied to nobler ends, including genuine rest, preparation, personal and family organization, self-improvement, and worship.

- *Achieving weightier things:* Right at the start of the week, you must reconnect with mission-vision goals and roles, and budget or allot time for the most important things to be done in the week and anchor them in a weekly diary. I shall illustrate this under the third principle.

Even though I could move on to discuss monthly and annual time management, these will be incorporated in "Making the Most of the Time" below to give room for a life-changing aspect of time management, which is managing time over a life span.

TIME MANAGEMENT OVER A LIFE SPAN. Martin Luther is reported to have said that he would live his life as if the Lord Jesus were coming today and yet would plant an apple tree. Those were the days when natural apple trees took years to mature and bear fruit. In other words, he would balance the short term with the long term.

I believe every Christian should have the same attitude. We do not know when Jesus will return or when we will die. Thus, we should make the most of every opportunity. At the same time, we must plan to live 70 to 80 years in accordance with the biblical parameters of life (Psalm 90:10). How long we actually live is for God to decide. Two of my mentors are Oswald Chambers, author of *My Utmost for His Highest,* and Billy Graham, probably the greatest evangelist of the 20th century. The first lived for a little over 40 years and the latter is still alive at 80-plus years at the time of writing. Each has greatly impacted the course of Christendom. It is not how long you live but how you live that matters. Those who make the most of their lives, however, often have a strategy for their whole life.

There is a second reason why looking over the whole spectrum of one's life is important. The preacher said, "There is a time for everything, and a season for every activity under heaven" (Ecclesiastes 3:1). For most people, each stage of life seems tailored to some particular achievements:

- *0-5 years* are wonderful for learning languages, internalizing basic social norms, and developing self-control.

- *6-12 years* are foundational years of learning life skills.

- *The teenage years* (or "the temporary madness period") seem particularly important for education and the formation of vocational skills.

- *Early adulthood* (20-plus to 30 years or thereabouts) is when most people complete college and make major decisions in life, such as career, marriage, and place of residence. These are the years in which those who missed out on advanced education can easily take remedial measures.

- *The middle years,* 30-plus to about 55, are great because they mark the period of greatest contribution to family, work, church, and society.

- *The mature years,* 55 to 70, are wonderful for consolidating leadership and gracefully passing the baton to the next generation and watching them take over! I have just entered that group, and I love it.

- *The twilight years* of 70-plus: Oh, how I love to be close to these senior citizens whose very jokes can be full of life-changing wisdom, the delight of grandchildren, a blessing to their grown-up sons and daughters. It is unfortunate that in our time three generations of families living together have become a thing of the past.

It is important at any stage of one's life to take a long-term view of the whole of life. You are likely to make wiser decisions and use your time better at each stage if you learn to number your days.

Principle 3: Making the Most of the Time

This principle is so important that most time-management techniques and books on time management focus solely on it. They fail, however, because they presuppose that what is needed foremost are tools and techniques to manage time, to the neglect of commitment to vision and values and the determination to make a difference in one's life.

Let me suggest some ideas for how you can make the most of your time.

NURTURING SPIRITUAL MATURITY. Set aside time for personal devotion (reading the Bible, meditating, and prayer), active participation in a Bible-believing church, being a witness for Jesus, and serving the Lord and the church in accordance with the gifts the Lord has given you.

CARE FOR MARRIAGE AND FAMILY. In Song of Songs, we meet the apt statement that they "made me take care of the vineyards; my own vineyard I have neglected" (Song of Songs 1:6). What a sad comment, and yet how true it is of many that their outside contribution is not matched by their care for those they claim to love the most. Does your calendar ever list time with your spouse and children, family anniversaries, vacation, or a visit to the ice cream parlour?

These are too important to be left to chance. You must budget time for them.

SELF-IMPROVEMENT. For many, studying ends with graduation from school or college. The Bible charges us always to study to show ourselves approved as workmen who have no need to be ashamed, rightly handling the word of truth (2 Timothy 2:15). You must budget your time for continuous study, reading classical Christian and non-Christian literature, and learning new skills and updating old ones. I must confess that in my case it has become a habit that I am always a student, studying for one certificated programme or another by distance and flexible learning.

DOES YOUR CALENDAR EVER LIST TIME WITH YOUR SPOUSE AND CHILDREN, FAMILY ANNIVERSARIES, VACATION, OR A VISIT TO THE ICE CREAM PARLOUR?

USING TIME MANAGEMENT TOOLS. I find myself returning to conventional time planners and diaries. These are useful tools, especially with the help of an able personal assistant in their difficult job of disciplining leaders to adhere to schedules, avoid overcommitments, and keep first things first. I thank God He created personal assistants. I call mine "the boss," for within set parameters, he has the authority to exercise discipline over me.

In actually managing your time, I recommend five tools, four of which are embodied in any good diary:

1) *The first,* which you have to create yourself, is your personal strategic plan and supporting management programme. No matter how long that document is—and it must always be written down—you must do a one-page summary to insert in the diary or keep in a conspicuous place for yourself. All other time-management frameworks must be driven by the personal strategic plan, because it is the achievement of the mission, vision, and goals that one must manage time to accomplish. (See chapter 4.)

2) *Annual Planner:* I like the one big sheet type that you can place on the wall. But any form that allows you to look at a whole year at a glance will do. Box 5.1 (page 94) is easy to create on a computer if you do not want to spend a few dollars to purchase one from the bookshop. It will serve the same purpose.

   On your annual planner, indicate all the important things you must undertake in a year—writing a book, going on vacation, attending a convention, etc. Some are standard; others will emerge as the year unfolds.

3) *Monthly Planner:* What is done for the year is repeated in detail for each month. A good diary should have a page for each month that allows the allocation of time for the most important things. Thus for February it may look like Box 5.2

	January	February	March	April	May	June	July	August	September	October	November	December
1												
2												
3												
4												
5												
6												
7												
8												
9												
10												
11												
12												
13												
14												
15												
16												
17												
18												
19												
20												
21												
22												
23												
24												
25												
26												
27												
28												
29												
30												
31												

BOX 5.1   DAYS ANNUAL PLANNER

(page 96). Once again block days you want to devote to certain important activities—a weekend with your spouse, attendance at Junior's graduation, board meetings, etc. Your annual planner can double as a monthly planner, too.

4) *Weekly Planner:* A major contribution of Stephen Covey is the concept of weekly time management driven by mission-vision roles and goals.[2] He recommends that at the beginning of the week you must budget time in line with your goals and roles for the important things to be accomplished in the week. I have practiced it for some time and found that if you take the initiative to put your important items on your weekly agenda (first things first), you will organize other things around your priorities and not vice versa. Using a weekly framework to organize immediate issues in one's life is a powerful instrument of purpose-driven time management. (See Box 5.3 on page 97).

IF YOU TAKE THE
INITIATIVE TO PUT YOUR
IMPORTANT ITEMS ON
YOUR WEEKLY AGENDA,
YOU WILL ORGANIZE
OTHER THINGS AROUND
YOUR PRIORITIES AND
NOT VICE VERSA.

The power of using the calendars is that they help you connect with your vision, goals, and roles and your weekly use of time. I advise you to spend time identifying the most impor-

BOX 5.2 MONTHLY TIMEFRAME FOR FEBRUARY						
SUNDAY	MONDAY	TUESDAY	WEDNESDAY	THURSDAY	FRIDAY	SATURDAY
1	2	3	4	5	6	7
8	9	10	11	12	13	14
15	16	17	18	19	20	21
22	23	24	25	26	27	28

tant things to be done in the week, and that must be anchored first. The rest of the time can be filled in as the week goes by. In so doing, what is important is set to be accomplished. My experience has shown that once that is done, there is still enough time to meet most other legitimate demands. The difference now is that the other demands are met on your terms.

5) *Daily Schedule:* This does not require much elaboration, for practically everyone is used to it. The most important thing is to anchor the two or three "must do" items for each day at the beginning of the week and to revisit them at the close of the preceding day or early in the morning. In my case, since I have to connect with my personal assistant at the close of each day, we have a one-page format in the computer in which all planned activities of the following day are summarized. Box 5.4 (page 98) is actually a reproduction of my daily schedule framework from the computer with a typical day's must do items.

BOX 5.3
WEEKLY TIME FRAME

	Sunday	Monday	Tuesday	Wednesday	Thursday	Friday	Saturday
5:00							
5:30							
6:00							
6:30							
7:00							
7:30							
8:00							
8:30							
9:00							
9:30							
10:00							
10:30							
11:00							
11:30							
12:00							
12:30							
1:00							
1:30							
2:00							
2:30							
3:00							
3:30							
4:00							
4:30							
5:00							
5:30							
6:00							
6:30							
7:00							
7:30							

Principle 4: Reckon with Time

You must hold yourself accountable for the use of your time. We all know what happens to most New Year's resolutions. They last only the first few days of the year. That is not what self-management is about. That is why we have stressed commitment, good habits, and discipline in earlier sections. You must put in place deadlines and target dates to accomplish short-, medium-, and long-term goals.

BOX 5.4
TODAY'S ACTIONS

DATE: _____

TIME	ACTIVITY	COMMENTS
8:00 a.m.	Operations Team Meeting	
8:30 a.m.		
9:00 a.m.	Opening Executive Masters Programme	
9:30 a.m.		
10:00 a.m.	Meeting Minister of Employment	
10:30 a.m.		
11:00 a.m.		
11:30 a.m.		
12:00 noon		
12:30 p.m.	Chair Management Board Meeting	
1:00 p.m.		
1:30 p.m.	Lunch with visitors from Birmingham University	
2:00 p.m.	Attending ABC Board Meeting	
2:30 p.m.		
3:00 p.m.		
3:30 p.m.		
4:00 p.m.		
4:30 p.m.		
5:00 p.m.		
5:30 p.m.		
6:00 p.m.	Address on Personal Financial Management at First Baptist Church	
7:00 p.m.		
7:30 p.m.	Dinner	
8:00 p.m.	Family Time	

The importance of writing down your plans, goals, and main tasks is to help implementation and monitoring. It may be in a notebook or on the wall. The most important thing is that they must be visible and inescapable, and S.M.A.R.T. (specific, measurable, attainable, realistic, and time-bound). You will need your written document to monitor progress and reckon with time use.

> THE IMPORTANCE OF WRITING DOWN YOUR PLANS, GOALS, AND MAIN TASKS IS TO HELP IMPLEMENTATION AND MONITORING.

Moreover, time must be set aside for formal monitoring and evaluation. Make it simple and fun, and organize it around family events. What better time to review your marriage than on a wedding anniversary? Or review your life goals than on birthdays? Or review your financial discipline than on paydays? Or review your family goals than in the relaxed atmosphere of annual holidays?

Few people are disciplined enough to implement self-accountability schemes by themselves. Consider employing the following five groups of allies to help you monitor and evaluate your progress. They are listed in order of importance to a family leader.

a) *Your wife*. She will want you to succeed, but not, however, at the expense of the marriage and the family.

b) *Your children*. Children will be among the first to detect imbalance in your life. And if you give them the opportunity to help you monitor progress, they will give neither you nor heaven rest until you do what is required. Give them the right to comment on your use of time. Many leaders do not know how important their success truly means to their followers, which, in the home, are their spouse and children.

c) *Your office assistant.* These may be called personal secretaries, executive assistants, or by some other nomenclature. The important thing is that such people help in organizing a leader's time and schedules. They are important in ensuring that important things are kept important, that appointments are kept, and that red flags are raised before ordinary things become urgent. They are a great help in discipline and time management. Be sure that times are blocked for leisure, rest, and whatever is necessary on your calendar. Then empower and train them to be wise and discriminatory in managing your calendar. After all, you are the boss, and ordinarily, the buck stops with you. So unless you delegate and empower others to help manage your time, they will do very little.

UNLESS YOU DELEGATE AND EMPOWER OTHERS TO HELP MANAGE YOUR TIME, THEY WILL DO VERY LITTLE.

d) *Reference or accountability group.* Every leader can do with a set of friends to whom he is accountable—friends who share his goals. This could be a cell group in the church, trusted friends at work, or old college mates who, thanks to the Internet, are just a click away.

e) *Mentors.* Everyone needs a mentor. I have mentors both alive and dead. The dead ones range from Paul and Peter to Martin Luther, E. Stanley Jones, and Oswald Chambers. They act as mentors to me as I read their writings. However, the mentors we are talking about here are those alive whom we look up to and whose views we respect. Give such people the liberty to comment on your progress and use of time. The Akans of Ghana have a proverb that says, "The path-maker scarcely sees whether the path he is making is crooked or straight." It pays to have a reference point.

BENEFITS OF THE ORGANIZED LIFE

The impact of the relatively well-organized life—not the perfect life, the pursuit of which may result in neurosis—is enormous. The rewards are many and significant. That is an illustration of the benefits of personal leadership. I list below some of the blessings of leading and managing your life as opposed to drifting.

By redeeming time, you have opportunity to increase skills and knowledge.
- Creativity is engendered as time is set aside for reflection.
- Enhanced productivity often results from increased skills and preparation.

- You need time for better social relationships with friends, and this comes by effective time management.

- Time for service to others is an important by-product of the organized life.

- Financial rewards often come in the wake of better time management.

- Spiritual growth is linked to your use of time.

- Better health may be the result of better organization of your life.

- Better family and marriage life is an important by-product of good time management.

- Time for leisure and recreation is more likely to be available.

QUESTIONS:

1. The author says, "Our vision, goals, and roles must drive our use of time and not vice versa." Why do you think this is so?

2. What daily demands take up most of your time? Do you see any way to change these?

3. What are some deliberate ways you can redeem time from your schedule?

4. God ordered man to take time to rest and recover. Why?

CHAPTER SIX

LEADING AT HOME I: KEY FUNCTIONS OF THE CHRISTIAN HOME

One of the weakest links in the literature on leadership has to do with leading at home. National and business leadership dominate leadership writings. This is characteristic of how much we have devalued the home—the mother of all institutions and the cradle of leadership.

Part of the problem, however, arises from the difference in nomenclature between business and home. Titles such as president, CEO, managing director, and mentor are not used at home—and rightly so. Instead, we talk about father, mother, and siblings. We cannot allow these names to mask the importance of the home as a major factor in shaping leadership in other spheres of life. There is no leader like a father or mother, husband or wife. The home is a place where all the challenges and functions of leadership are tested to the core and where, unfortunately, some fail miserably.

For one, most leaders will admit that much of what they are was learned at home. In my case, there is no doubt that I owe most to my visionary, enterprising, and, in some ways, disciplinarian mother, Abena Pomaa, who gave her seven sons dreams, vision, and what it takes to be a leader, despite her own handicap as an illiterate, poor, African rural farmer. The result is that she raised leaders in medicine, academia, and teaching in a traditionalist, male chauvinist society. This is because she was herself a true citizen leader. She gave us vision to struggle to be educated, to work hard, and to do everything with excellence. While Mum was exceptional, and I guess many readers will say the same about their parents, every parent is a leader in the home.

One of the difficult principles to get couples to understand is that it is important to manage their families consciously instead of allowing tradition and custom to guide them. Unfortunately, the very concept of a Christian home is not that obvious to many today. In this chapter, therefore, I will describe what I mean by the Christian home and its core functions. I have my wife to thank for many of these ideas.

THE CHRISTIAN HOME

It is important for us to start our discussion from first principles and define the Christian home and its functions. This is an age when the word *Christian* is often used to mean "good," "civilized," or even "Western." Christianity could be any of these, but it is more than that. Needless to say, a Christian home is a home that is "of Christ" in four ways.

First, it means the family relates to Jesus Christ as Saviour, whom they trust as a Redeemer. Second, and as a natural derivative of the above, the norms of the Bible (the Word and will of God) constitute the rule of life and conduct in that home. The third is that the lordship of Jesus Christ is celebrated in the sense that He is actively acknowledged as Head and Lord to be obeyed in family life. Finally, the members of the family are brought up in the "fear and admonition of God."

The Christian home performs five irreplaceable functions in the lives of its members and society:

- a place of worship

- an abiding place of love

- a school of learning

- a laboratory of work

- a place of governance

The Christian home is a place of worship

The Christian home is the nucleus of the church. If Jesus Christ is the Head, Lord, and Saviour of the Christian home, then the first function of the Christian home is worship. The irony today is that many Christians see the church as the place of worship in the same way as they expect Sunday school to be responsible for the spiritual upbringing of their children. That is contrary to the divine order.

THIS IS AN AGE WHEN THE WORD "CHRISTIAN" IS OFTEN USED TO MEAN "GOOD," "CIVILIZED," OR EVEN "WESTERN." CHRISTIANITY COULD BE ANY OF THESE, BUT IT IS MORE THAN THAT.

The home is to be a place where we learn holiness and worship, with the church serving as a forum for the collective celebration of our individual experiences. When we come together as a church, we are to come with a song in our mouths, a word of testimony or a psalm in our hearts brought from the home (Ephesians 5:19). In many cases people leading worship *at* church are tempted to use all manner of tricks to bring people to a worshipful mood after a week-long lack of vital Christianity in the home. If success in our spiritual life comes by reading the Bible and meditating on it "day and night," then it must be done in the home! (See Joshua 1:8.) In Deuteronomy 6:5-9 the saints are called upon to:

Love the LORD your God with all your heart and with all your soul and with all your strength. These commandments that I give you today are to be upon your hearts. Impress them on your children. Talk about them when you sit at home and when you walk along the road, when you lie down and when you get up. Tie them as symbols on your hands and bind them on your foreheads. Write them on the doorframes of your houses and on your gates.

If true religion starts from the heart, then the epicenter of its practice is in the home. If a family spends 30 minutes a day in prayer, Bible study, and worship, they would be spending about four times the time many spend in corporate worship. That would facilitate Christian growth and maturity more than what the church may do in one hour. Moreover, the church in the home facilitates practical religion and combines faith with living. Most important, the larger church will be stronger as a result of functional "churches" in homes.

The home is an abiding place of love

Total love is learned in the home. For one, it is only in the home that all aspects of love can be practised. First, romantic sexual love, *eros,* is to be practised among God's people within marriage alone. Then there is friendship, or *philos,* in the form of care, commitment, and sensitivity, as well as unconditional love. Most often, when people have relational problems in their marriage, at work, or with friends, they can be traced to a dysfunctional home life, where love is not known in its fullness.

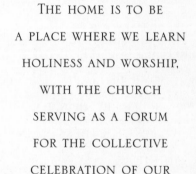

THE HOME IS TO BE A PLACE WHERE WE LEARN HOLINESS AND WORSHIP, WITH THE CHURCH SERVING AS A FORUM FOR THE COLLECTIVE CELEBRATION OF OUR INDIVIDUAL EXPERIENCES.

The function of the Christian home in teaching and practising love is irreplaceable. From the home we learn how to marry, how to live with others, and how to serve. This is because God intended the home to be the abiding place of love.

The home is a school of learning

The home is a school of learning whether the parents are conscious of it or not. In the home, a child will learn about faith, language, social norms, beliefs, and values. Between five and seven years of age, much of what the child will become is set on course. It amases me how a child born to a Chinese family in two years learns Chinese and by five has learned more than 75 percent of the norms of the Chinese people. An American child equally learns American English and culture. In the same way a Zulu child behaves like a Zulu that early. That is the power of the home in its impact on the intellectual, social, and spiritual development of people.

THE FUNCTION OF THE CHRISTIAN HOME IN TEACHING AND PRACTISING LOVE IS IRREPLACEABLE. FROM THE HOME WE LEARN HOW TO MARRY, HOW TO LIVE WITH OTHERS, AND HOW TO SERVE.

Besides the impact of the home atmosphere on learning, many a time the status and resources of the family also shape much of the forces that impact us. These include the neighbourhood we live in, the schools we attend, and friends we make. This is not to place undue emphasis on the environment. I do not believe in environmental determinism, which others use as an escape from personal responsibility. However, the impact of the home is so great that it becomes the dominant factor in our lives. Thus, a breakdown of social norms always starts with a breakdown of family life in the home.

The home is a laboratory of work

The school system is good at preparing people to be nurses, doctors, engineers, teachers, and farmers. But it is generally poor at teaching work ethics, personal organization, time management, and a yearning for quality and excellence.

We have found that, for example, when children are not taught at home to work with their hands, head, and heart, they are handicapped forever. Working with the hands—doing manual work, cleaning the house, learning to cook, washing the car—is so important for character and wholesome living that we are inclined to raise it a close second to personal Bible study and prayer. In this regard, today's youth are missing out on an important aspect of life with the increasing automation of family chores.

There is no better place to teach work habits than in the home, at the feet of Mum and Dad. The good thing is that most children love to work on the car with Dad, cook with parents, help in the home, or cut the grass. Their zeal and enthusiasm are likely to be dampened, however, by time-strapped parents who want to get through such chores with a zap. In that case, children are denied the opportunity to work with their hands. As a result, we have seen some young ladies go into panic when they are about to get married because they cannot figure out how to keep house.

The school system does a relatively good job in training people to work with the head. In fact, that is about all it is good at in many places. Home is where we need to learn the value of working with the heart—that is, developing a positive and healthy attitude to work.

RESPECT FOR AUTHORITY, MENTORING (WHICH PARENTING IS, TO A LARGE EXTENT), AND DISCIPLINE BEGIN AT HOME.

The home is a place of governance

The home is designed to train people to respect and live under authority and with others in harmony and mutual self-respect. We believe that the Bible, in naming the husband as the head in a two-member marriage unit, was resolving a governance issue. It does not imply the intrinsic superiority of one sex above the other. (More on that in chapter 8, "Leading One's Wife.")

The concept of governance is particularly important for the children. Respect for authority, mentoring (which parenting is, to a large extent), and discipline begin at home. When the home defaults on these functions, society pays a heavy price. It is in the home that we first learn the art of living with others, and to share common space, resources, hope, and aspirations.

The home is the cradle of leadership training. Children look up to their parents and imitate them. Thank God sometimes children from dysfunctional homes turn their backs on their parents' practices and learn better in later life. Generally, however, "like father like son" is a truism.

YOUR LEADERSHIP AT HOME COUNTS

Given the importance of the home in the lives of individuals, in families, and in society, it is unfortunate that leadership at home has not received the needed attention in the leadership literature. Of course, writing on parenting indirectly has to do with leadership. However, lack of explicit treatment of this important and most prevalent leadership role is inexplicable.

Within the context of the home, the apostle Paul warns parents in Ephesians 6:4 not to exasperate their children with unduly high expectations and demands, which is an admonition against high-handed, autocratic leadership. Unconsciously, you may be practising transactional quid pro quo leadership that commands followership only because you rely mainly on coercive power, be it physical, financial, or any other advantage you have.

The model of transformational servant leaders is most needed in the home, where the husband-father leads his family with a unique combination of humility, competence, character, and a self-sacrificing service, as Christ did for His bride, the church.

The type of home leadership that is both Christian and transforming stands in contrast to two of the most popular concepts of leadership, namely, traditional chauvinist male leadership and its ecclesiastical version of authoritarianism, which seem to pass readily with a veneer of theology. Let me illustrate the former from traditional African societies, where I grew up, which to a lesser degree seems to prevail in many other societies.

In traditional societies the husband is a patriarch, and that is evident in ancient Israelite society as reflected in the Pentateuch. The wife is definitely of a lower status. She is there to serve the husband—cook for him, care for his children, do most of the household chores, and meet his sexual needs.

In my traditional society, it is not uncommon to meet a man returning from the farm with his pregnant wife after a long day in the field. The woman may be carrying their youngest child on her back. She will be carrying the farm produce on her head for the evening meal, including the firewood for cooking the meal. Behind her will be her able-bodied husband, whistling joyously, holding his machete or gun, which weighs a lot less than the woman's load. On their arrival at home, the man relaxes in the chair while the wife boils water for him to bathe and prepares food for him. Later in the evening, the woman has sex with him. Such a relationship is approved by tradition, "the gods," and ancestors. In fact, it becomes so normative that a man who attempts to help the wife is ridiculed as having become a

THE MODEL OF TRANSFORMATIONAL SERVANT LEADERS IS MOST NEEDED IN THE HOME, WHERE THE HUSBAND-FATHER LEADS HIS FAMILY WITH A UNIQUE COMBINATION OF HUMILITY, COMPETENCE, CHARACTER, AND A SELF-SACRIFICING SERVICE, AS CHRIST DID FOR HIS BRIDE, THE CHURCH.

woman. Even the women folk may chastise the wife for making a woman out of him. While the above practice is extreme, many women all over the world complain of similar inequities, especially in undertaking household chores.

Sad to say, the verses used to justify that approach are the sacred words of apostle Paul:

Submit to one another out of reverence for Christ. Wives, submit to your husbands as to the Lord. For the husband is the head of the wife as Christ is the head of the church, his body, of which he is the Savior. Now as the church submits to Christ, so also wives should submit to their husbands in everything. Husbands, love your wives, just as Christ loved the church and gave himself up for her to make her holy, cleansing her by the washing with water through the word, and to present her to himself as a radiant church, without stain or wrinkle or any other blemish, but holy and blameless. In this same way, husbands ought to love their wives as their own bodies. He who loves his wife loves himself. After all, no one ever hated his own body, but he feeds and cares for it, just as Christ does the church—for we are members of his body. For this reason a man will leave his father and mother and be united to his wife, and the two will become one flesh. (Ephesians 5:21-31)

One wonders how these verses could be used to support any kind of male leadership other than a servant leader. For one, both the man and the woman are charged as brethren to submit or yield ground to each other whenever issues of godliness, obedience, or reverence to Christ are involved (v. 21). The man is to be the head of, or leader of, his wife. But the parameters are clear: "as Christ is the head of the church," to "love [agape, or self-sacrificing, unconditional love] as Christ loved the church and gave himself up for her" (v. 25), to "love their wives as their own bodies" (v. 29). Verse 31 gives the reason why a man is to leave his father and mother and cleave to his wife—and that is to love her till the two are one in spirit, soul, and body.

> MALE LEADERSHIP IN THE HOME IS TO BE CHRISTLIKE, LOVING, AND SELF-SACRIFICING.

Male leadership in the home is to be Christlike, loving, and self-sacrificing. I believe that if Christian male leadership is of the kind the Bible prescribes, submission of the wife will almost invariably be automatic, for it would be to her highest advantage to do so.

The Bible clearly states that the kind of husband-father leader that is required in the Christian home is the one that Christ modeled. In Mark 10:42-45, Jesus stated how different our leadership must be:

You know that those who are regarded as rulers of the Gentiles lord it over them, and their high officials exercise authority over them. Not so with you. Instead, whoever wants to become great among you must be your servant, and whoever wants to be first must be slave of all. For even the Son of Man did not come to be served, but to serve, and to give his life as a ransom for many.

And He went on to demonstrate servant leadership on the night of His crucifixion by washing the feet of His disciples when no servant was around and no disciple was willing to stoop so low as to do the work of a servant. When He was finished He said:

You call me "Teacher" and "Lord," and rightly so, for that is what I am. Now that I, your Lord and Teacher, have washed your feet, you also should wash one another's feet. I have set you an example that you should do as I have done for you. I tell you the truth, no servant is greater than his master, nor is a messenger greater than the one who sent him. Now that you know these things, you will be blessed if you do them. (John 13:13-17)

QUESTIONS:

1. What are the key functions of the Christian home?

2. Why must we recover the original meaning of the word *Christian?*

3. Where should a child receive his primary spiritual training? Why?

4. Do you and your wife model good Christian habits in the home? Is there a way you can improve on this?

CHAPTER SEVEN

LEADING AT HOME II: THE PRACTICE AND CHALLENGES

Nowhere is effective leadership needed more than in the home where young lives are moulded. This is because effective leaders perform the following functions, which are irreplaceable:

- *Provide direction.* This you do by defining purpose, the vision, and specific goals to work toward. The home often is where dreams, vision, and aspiration are inculcated.

- *Develop strategies.* This brings about the vision. Strategies need to take account of the development of each member of the family, especially the mother, whose personal development is often sacrificed.

- *Mobilize followers.* That translates into rallying the family members by inspiring, motivating, and empowering them toward vision realization.

- *Manage change.* This you do through helping the family cope with the many transitions of marriage and the growth of children into independent adults, including the turbulent and "mad" teen years. If anyone thinks managing change in a company and institution is more difficult, he most likely has not taken seriously the job of managing the economic, social, spiritual, and physical changes in the home. I call it the world's greatest job.

> NOWHERE IS
> EFFECTIVE LEADERSHIP
> NEEDED MORE THAN
> IN THE HOME
> WHERE YOUNG LIVES
> ARE MOULDED.

- *Lead in decision making and problem solving.* This is required not just in financial matters, but also with spiritual and social issues.

- *Develop other leaders.* Help members of the family, from toddlers to one's spouse, to realize their God-given potential to influence others and their world for good.

THE CONTEXT OF LEADERSHIP IN THE HOME

While leadership principles cut across different contexts—the home, school, community, business and institutions, and society at large—the particular context is important in shaping the right leadership. Moreover, follower characteristics and maturity are of great significance. It is therefore essential for us to note three important features of the home context that ought to impact leadership and the application of the above functions in the home. These are first, the *loving* consanguine context. The second has to do with the unique *conjugal* relationship of the husband and wife. The third has to do with the *parent-child* relationship.

It is so easy to reduce male leadership in the home to the provision of a roof over the head, transportation, and school fees to see junior through college. A husband and father has to do all that, but so can the state. The father must be physically there to give a hug, play with junior, and to give support for homework, and these cannot be delegated.

When it comes to leading at home, many men don't understand that it is a partnership calling with the wife. The Bible is clear on that. It is "the two," not one and a half, that become one. Malachi 2:14 states, "She is your partner, the wife of your marriage covenant." God made her a "helper suitable for him" (Genesis 2:18). Understanding the concept of partnership is significant to understanding male leadership at home. It is the equivalent of being the president of a professional association whereby one is *primus inter pares* (first among equals). The same applies when it comes to leading your wife.

In her book *The Joy of Human Love,* my wife, Georgina, introduced a concept that has become a standard feature of all our subsequent work on family life. She outlines three things that should form the basis of the relationship between Christian spouses and that should engender mutual respect and recognition of their roles as partners.

First, the husband and the wife are equal. They were equally made in the image of God (Genesis 1:26-27), they are equal in sin (Genesis 3; Romans 3:23), and they are equal in redemption (Galatians 3:28). The champions of the women's liberation movement should be able to say amen to that.

> THE MOST IMPORTANT FACTOR IN YOUR HOME LEADERSHIP IS YOU — YOUR CHARACTER, YOUR CARE, YOUR SUBMISSION TO CHRIST.

But equality is not the end. Male and female in Christ are equal but different. The physical, psychological, and emotional differences between men and women are incontrovertible. It would seem that even their spiritual responses are different.

The good news is that much of the differences between the sexes are designed by God to complement each other as partners or, better still, "joint heirs." The holistic intuition of most women versus the logical thinking of many men, the unique sex organs of men and women, and many other differences are all divinely ordained to complement each other.

Developing an appreciation of the sexes as equal, different, and complementary will build each other up, especially the wife's self-esteem; engender mutual respect; and put the leadership role of the man within its proper context. It is leadership in partnership, and partners work together as a team.

The importance of partnership in home leadership stems from the fact that in relation to children, both the husband, as leader, and the wife, as partner, are also parents. The children must therefore grow up giving equal honour to Mum and Dad. Thus, in exercising his leadership function, the husband must in no way devalue the authority of the wife in the eyes of the children. On the contrary, as the man provides Christlike leadership to his wife by serving, respecting, and sensitively and unconditionally seeking what is best for her, he will be giving a priceless gift to his children—love of their mum. The greatest thing a man can do for his children is to love their mum, his wife!

THE PRACTICE OF LEADING AT HOME

Husbands and fathers must aim at building a winning family team. Obvious as that may seem, the conscious practical application of leadership principles to the home is so rare that I will use this section to indicate what it entails in practice.

I need to caution you at the outset, however. You can become paranoid and rigid with leadership at home and begin writing tonnes of family strategic plans. That will not help and, in all probability, neither your spouse nor children are likely to be interested in that. Try to read a lengthy family budget to your 7-year-old child and you will be met with yawns (except if there is a line item on pocket money and it comes up early). Instead, use the following suggestions to orient your thinking and foster better exercise of leadership at home.

Make yourself a person others can honour and follow with respect. The most important factor in your home leadership is you—your character, your care, your submission to Christ. Remember, as a husband you are an under-shepherd of Christ. It is His flock you are called to lead. Thus, leading yourself is a prerequisite for effective leadership at home. A leader is a person others want to follow willingly without violation of their individual freedom or self-worth. In that regard, leadership has to be earned.

Clarify and/or develop a family mission. Encourage your household to clarify its mission as a Christian family. This is particularly important, as practising Christian family life in a materialistic, godless society will force you to face serious challenges. This is where Joshua of old is our best example. He told the Israelites to make a choice whether they would serve other gods or Yahweh. He added, "As for me and my household, we will serve the Lord" (Joshua 24:15). Unless your family can unashamedly say that, you are likely to cave in as the pressures mount to keep up with the Joneses. In the same way as Joshua, Jeremiah, and Daniel stood up for godliness when all around them was a sea of immorality, idolatry, and godlessness, our families can also stand up for godliness if they know that to "fear God and keep his commandments . . . is the whole duty of man" (Ecclesiastes 12:13). The husband-father must model the fear of God.

Set a vision that captivates, energizes, and mobilizes. Your family mission should drive your vision, which must be couched in a way that is intelligible to all members of the family. For example, Colossians 1:28 is a good vision for Christian families: To "present every [member of the family] perfect [or mature] in Christ." That is what our labours should be directed at. Maturity entails balance, discernment, and right judgment in the physical, social, intellectual, and spiritual realms. Hard as it may be, as early as possible each member of the family must be encouraged to develop his or her own vision, not necessarily to be a doctor, lawyer, or teacher, but to be a mature servant of Christ in any particular sphere of service the Lord leads him or her.

Develop clear, simple, measurable, attainable, realistic, and time-bound goals for the family. The family must have clear goals for each of the important areas of the family and the individual lives, such as spiritual development, intellectual growth, and judgment. The family must set itself financial goals, social goals, and physical-growth goals, especially for the children. In that regard, housewives are often the first casualties of the lack of specific goals for family members. The children tend to become the focus of all attention till they leave home. In some cases, the result is that by the time mother is in her 50s and the husband has become significant in business or ministry, with the children having become doctors and engineers, mother still remains the high school graduate she was. She would have given all she had and become an empty shell because there was no plan for her progress for the 20 to 30 years she may still live after her child-rearing years!

Work together to elaborate how each of the goals can be realized.
That is all that strategies are about—the how-to of vision attainment. Let me illustrate. I was determined that the high potential
of Georgina should be fully realized because she has even greater
potential to contribute to the church and society after the kids
leave home. She was therefore persuaded, and it took a lot of loving persuasion, to get her to register to go back to school. Without
a conscious effort and careful selec-
tion of programmes that allow her
to study and at the same time take
care of the family, this dream would
not have been realized.

> LEADERS MAJOR ON
> INSPIRING, MOTIVATING,
> ENCOURAGING, AND
> EMPOWERING
> FOLLOWERS—IN THIS
> CASE WIVES
> AND CHILDREN—
> TO DEVELOP THEIR
> FULLEST POTENTIAL.

In the same way, for each goal
and for each member of the family,
the leader, with his family, must
elaborate what will be required to
meet the targets, taking account of
the internal and external resources
and constraints on the family. That
is the essence of strategy. You must,
however, distinguish between coercion and motivation. The leader
is to get others to achieve great things through inspiration, motivation, and encouragement, and not by force or dictation.

Put together a simple family-development plan. We encourage families to write down in simple outline what Georgina and I
call in our book *Manual for Family Life Counseling* a "Family

Development Plan." It always helps to put down your mission, vision, goals, and strategies, however simple form it takes. And put your plan in a place you are likely to visit often as a family.

Mobilize family members to implement the strategy in pursuit of vision attainment. Leaders major on inspiring, motivating, encouraging, and empowering followers—in this case wives and children—to develop their fullest potential. It is important not to concentrate only on the extroverts in the home. Each member requires the leader's special attention as a unique individual. Mobilization is a central leadership function. Others must see themselves as part of the vision. They must buy into the strategies and be motivated to rise and build a unique family "cathedral" where Christ is honoured.

Resource mobilization. It is the responsibility of the leader in the home to identify the resources needed for the family's growth. And here men are likely to focus on the financial and material aspects to the neglect of other equally important areas. Does a child need a specialist in education? Do you put enough thought into the choice of school or place of worship? Is enough attention being devoted to family togetherness? The tendency is to leave such matters to the mother. The leader leads his family. Even if you delegate sometimes (and that is part of leading), interest and responsibility should not be abandoned.

Manage family transitions carefully. Families go through many transitions—a move to new places and/or jobs, going through seasons of marriage, children growing from childhood through teenage years

> WE MUST,
> AS CHRISTIAN
> MALE LEADERS,
> BE ASKING AND
> TRUSTING JESUS TO
> GIVE US WISDOM
> AND GUIDANCE.

to adulthood. These are inevitable transitions that the leader of the home has to oversee and manage with care and commitment. For example, the wife often needs exceptional support through her menopause. But some husbands are too busy with corporate or church/ministry responsibilities to even take notice of "Mummy's mad days."

God of our fathers in whom we trust. Last but not least, leading your family requires faith in God. We must, as Christian male leaders, be asking and trusting Jesus to give us wisdom and guidance. It is the responsibility of the father to offer sacrifices. Today, we do not need the blood of bulls, because Christ has sacrificed His blood once and for all for us. Nonetheless, we have to offer prayers and intercession for each member of the family.

OBSTACLES TO EFFECTIVE MALE LEADERSHIP AT HOME

I will conclude this chapter with reference to some obstacles that men are likely to face in seeking to provide effective leadership at home:

- Men's constitution
- Sin as expressed in selfishness

- Tradition
- Confusion regarding the status of the sexes
- Misinterpretation of some key scriptures
- Ignorance of the tools of effective leadership
- Satan

Men's constitution. Men, by nature, seem constitutionally biased to fight it out, dominate, and demand respect for their leadership. This tendency is a major obstacle to effective servant leadership at home. It has been manifested in our nature since Adam and Eve sinned (the Fall). Ever since the Fall, we have been likely, even if in the wrong, to point fingers at "the woman you put here with me" (see Genesis 3:12). This is where we must learn to "submit to one another out of reverence for Christ" (Ephesians 5:21).

Sin as expressed in selfishness. The worst part of this bent is that at the office, men accept their female colleagues as equal partners, listen to them, and even receive orders from them if the female happens to be a senior or supervisor. Yet the same man at home wants to have the last word, win every argument, and dominate.

A worst-case scenario involved Joe and Christie (not their real names). Christie was a medical doctor. Joe did not have a college degree. Joe was so paranoid that he went out of his way to make unreasonable demands on Christie, and, but for the grace of God and her longsuffering, their marriage would have ended in divorce.

The answer to this is to learn of Jesus, who says, "I am meek and humble." An enemy of Christian marriage, and by extension the family, is sin as expressed in selfishness. Self-interest will undermine every leadership situation, and the home is not an exception. Selfishness is often expressed in the desire to have one's needs met at the expense of others. In marriage this manifests itself particularly in the bedroom, where men often seek sexual satisfaction with little regard to the needs of their wives. The reality is that men do not have a monopoly on selfishness; in the case of women, selfishness often takes the form of subtle manipulation. We need not talk about children who, when younger, often appear to be a bundle of selfishness. We must acknowledge selfishness in us as sin and something to repent of and confess to Jesus to be forgiven. With the help of the Holy Spirit we must overcome this tendency. And this is not a one-off exercise. We are to continue until, like our Lord, we can say, "I am among you as one who serves."

SELFISHNESS IS OFTEN EXPRESSED IN THE DESIRE TO HAVE ONE'S NEEDS MET AT THE EXPENSE OF OTHERS.

Tradition. Invariably, our tradition, wherever we come from, is tainted by sin and, as a consequence, does not support the kind of servant leader Scripture advocates. As in other areas of our Christian life, Jesus confronts us: "You have let go of the commands of God and are holding on to the traditions of men" (Mark 7:8). Every human tradition has some good aspects that conform to the will of God, a residue of God having made us in His nature. But there are parts of our tradition that reflect our rebellion, too.

We are to let Christ and His Word judge our traditions and not vice versa. It is only when we can say "we must obey God rather than men" (Acts 5:29) that we are truly conformed to His image.

For example, in some traditional societies the spouses still remain members of their respective extended families. Their children therefore belong to the woman's family and not to the man's, or vice versa. This is diametrically opposed to the biblical concept of the "two become one flesh." In the same way, it is becoming frequent for couples in Western societies to sign premarital contracts regarding how they will share property should the marriage end in divorce. In other words, no longer is marriage for better for worse till death, but for as long as we agree for it to last.

None of us is culturally neutral, even though some seem to think so. We invariably substitute one culture or tradition with another because we are social beings. Thus the question is which traditions we will keep and which ones we will discard. I advise Christians that after discarding the Jewish sociocultural context of biblical teaching, there still remains a distinctly biblical worldview (beliefs and assumptions that are at the makeup of a culture) that you must adopt. In the case of leadership, it has been repeated again and again that the biblical model is servant leadership, and the example is Jesus Himself. Thus you have to examine His culture and decide to adopt the biblical pattern where there is a conflict.

Confusion regarding the status of the sexes. We live in an age when the push for gender equality in its worst form is being interpreted to mean there are no differences between men and women. Visiting Kenya in June 2003, I was interested to hear that a new draft constitution would eliminate reference to the husband as the head of the home. While we should support the elimination of gender discrimination, it should not be at the expense of the clear teachings of the Word of God—that men and women are equal but different. They were created to perform complementary roles, which should be the basis of mutual respect and admiration. In Christ, each should be able to say, "I am fearfully and wonderfully made" (Psalm 139:14).

> MUCH CONFUSION ARISES WITH REGARD TO THE EXACT MEANING OF THE COMMAND FOR WIVES TO SUBMIT TO THEIR HUSBANDS.

Understanding the status of the sexes in marriage is very important to leadership in the home. If men and women are equal, different, and complementary, then not only is male leadership that of a servant, but it is also exercised with the wife as a partner. That way, there will be mutual respect and support to ensure that the family enterprise succeeds.

Among genuine Bible-believing Christians, one challenge to servant leadership comes from misinterpretation of certain portions of Scripture, particularly Ephesians 5:22-23 and analogous passages that seem to suggest that the woman is subordinate, even inferior, to the man. In particular, much confusion arises with regard to the exact meaning of the command for wives to submit to their husbands. In fact, until recently, when women began to mount the pulpit, one heard many sermons about submission of wives to their husbands and very little on male servant leadership. Even when people talked about the man as the head of his wife, the clear inference to sacrificial and unconditional love was glossed over. Instead, the emphasis was on the need for wives to submit because the husband is the head.

My advice is that a male servant leader should be less concerned about the wife obeying God and concentrate on his own responsibilities of unconditional love, nurturing of his wife, clinging to her, and living with her in knowledge. If you do this, almost invariably the wife will respect you (Ephesians 5:25-33; 1 Peter 3:7). If he is a leader, as he leads she will follow.

Ignorance of the tools of effective leadership. Sometimes the problem with effective servant leadership has to do with this ignorance. Even though we spend several years at college to learn our various professions, some actually enter marriage without any preparation other than observing their parents' marriage and what they can figure out through magazines and newspapers. I trust that this book highlights the tools for effective male leadership in the home. The Bible, however, remains the major sourcebook on leadership at home. Other excellent books on being a husband and father include those written by James Dobson, Gordon MacDonald, Chuck Swindoll, and J. Oswald Sanders.

Satan. Last but not the least, Satan will attack governance in the home, especially a home that is dedicated to honouring God. That was what Adam ignored, and he fell as a result. And instead of repenting of his sin and asking for forgiveness, Adam resorted to accusing his wife—and God. The first male leadership failure was therefore in the Garden of Eden. The whole of human history would be different today if he had exercised leadership. The Bible calls on us to "resist the devil, and he will flee from you" and to keep him at bay by drawing near to God (James 4:7-8).

> THE FIRST MALE LEADERSHIP FAILURE WAS THEREFORE IN THE GARDEN OF EDEN.

In conclusion, I want to emphasize that most men, especially Christian men, will lead their families better if they:

- Acknowledge the importance of their family to its members.

- Accord the home the priority that God expects us to give.

- Learn to apply the principles of effective leadership to their homes.

- Focus on confronting the challenges to being effective leaders at home.

Our families are not looking for angels. They will want to follow our leadership as they see, hear, and feel what the leader *does* more than what he says.

QUESTIONS:

1. What are the irreplaceable functions of the Christian home?

2. How is the leader-follower relationship different in varying contexts, e.g., home, church, and business?

3. Why is it important that followers respect their leaders?

4. What are some of the obstacles to male leadership in the home?

CHAPTER EIGHT

LEADING ONE'S WIFE

Leading your wife is a unique leadership challenge. This is because unlike other situations, it involves leadership within a partnership. It may be compared to the position of a managing partner in a two-member firm. Moreover, the basis of a male leader and his wife is to be modeled after that of Christ and His church. To understand male leadership within such a partnership, it is equally important that we first explore biblically defined parameters of marriage as God intended it. Within that framework, we must seek to understand the responsibilities of the spouses.

Marriage, as God intended it, is a covenantal relationship between one man and one woman for life. As such, it behooves us to outline briefly the type of partnership that must characterize Christian marriage. A forthcoming book written by Georgina and me is titled *God's Master Plan for Christian Marriage*. It provides greater detail on marriage as God intended it to be, the outline of which is sketched below.

GOD'S PLAN FOR CHRISTIAN MARRIAGE

It is amazing how few people, even committed Christians, think through marriage as God intended it. Occasionally, we have asked the attendees at our seminars, "How do you marry as a Christian?" By their responses it is apparent that as important as most Christians consider marriage, they have only fuzzy ideas as to what Christian marriage is all about. Yet Amos 3:3 says, "Do two walk together unless they have agreed to do so?" So one wonders what couples agree to in marriage. It becomes scary if two people vow "for better for worse, for richer for poorer" without knowing what the partnership entails.

> MARRIAGE, AS GOD INTENDED IT, IS A COVENANTAL RELATIONSHIP BETWEEN ONE MAN AND ONE WOMAN FOR LIFE.

Marriage may be looked at from seven angles: mission, foundation, cultivation, product, duration, partners, and responsibilities. I will elaborate on each briefly before highlighting a few challenges and three enemies to this divine plan for Christian marriage:

The Purpose or Mission of Marriage as God Intended

In a world where everything is becoming relative and happiness is being made an end in itself, it is important to reaffirm that marriage was God's idea from the beginning, and He created it to fulfill His purposes, which may be summarized as follows:

To bring glory to God. There is nothing Christian that is not directed at glorifying God. In fact, marriage is the one social institution out of which all other social structures have evolved. It is important to appreciate the mission of marriage as a means to honour God and bring praise to His name. This appreciation alters one's attitude fundamentally. In other words, my joy and happiness are important by-products of my marriage but not the ultimate goal of Christian marriage.

To provide companionship to each other. One of the fundamental purposes of marriage is companionship. God created Eve because "it is not good for the man to be alone" (Genesis 2:18). Psalm 68:6 says, "God sets the lonely in families." This mission of biblical marriage is often downplayed during the course of many a marriage to the detriment of the couple. Sometimes that occurs for apparently good reasons, such as care for children, the pursuit of career or money, and even Christian service. But if the companionship and friendship of the couple are neglected, the consequences are always grave for the relationship, especially in their old age when career and children are gone. Thus, with the organization of modern work and, sometimes, the inevitable need for the partners to work outside the home, Christian couples must consciously create time to be together for fellowship, companionship, and friendship.

To minister to each other. Not only was it not good for the man to be alone, he needed a helper. Marriage is meant to create helpmates to meet the needs of each other. Each spouse has needs that God intends to be met in marriage. While in some ways some of the needs can be met in other social relationships, the deep social, emotional, and physical needs can be met only in a marital relationship. Human beings see themselves in social relationships, and marriage is the most intimate of all the social relationships. In his book *The Marriage Builder,* Lawrence J. Crabb, Jr. emphasizes that true marriage is a means of affirming our sense of significance. To that end, the spouse plays the role of a minister.

WHILE SOME OF THE NEEDS CAN BE MET IN OTHER SOCIAL RELATIONSHIPS, THE DEEP SOCIAL, EMOTIONAL, AND PHYSICAL NEEDS CAN BE MET ONLY IN A MARITAL RELATIONSHIP.

To procreate godly offspring. The procreation function was at the core of God's purpose in creating the first man and woman. He commanded them to be fruitful, multiply, and fill the earth—something we have done very well. But the biblical mission to have children goes beyond the physical act of having babies. It calls for the raising of godly children, and the Christian marriage creates the ideal loving, nurturing atmosphere for doing so.

To create the basic unit for work and service. Christian couples are to serve God together, raise godly children, keep house, and minister in the church and the community.

The Bible says two are better than one (Ecclesiastes 4:9) and that there is effectual power in two praying together (Matthew 18:19-20). It is easy to overlook the fact that when the Bible talks about "two or three" praying together, that applies equally to a Christian couple. I call it the "couple power" of Christian marriage. And that power is to be harnessed to impact our children, our church, and our community through work and service.

The foundation of marriage: transformed relationships

This and the next two elements in God's master plan for marriage derive from Genesis 2:24-25, which is repeated four times in the Bible: "Therefore shall a man leave his father and his mother, and shall cleave unto to his wife: and they shall be one flesh. And they were naked, the man and his wife, and were not ashamed" (KJV).

Biblical marriage starts with "leaving" (the foundation), is sustained by "cleaving" (the process), and results in one flesh (the product). Leaving implies a radical transformation of the basic and strongest premarital relationship, that between the man and woman and their respective parents, and by extension all other relationships. The Bible does not advocate abandonment of one's parents and relatives to marry (1 Timothy 5:8). Rather, it expects a radical transformation of the parent-child relationship so that a new unit is formed through marriage.

It is important for a newlywed couple to realize that it is in their interest to change their relationship with their parents. The root of many bad relations with in-laws can often be traced to either the parents or the children not being able to transform their relationship at the time of marriage to facilitate the bonding of the couple to be one flesh. The foundation of Christian marriage is this transformation. In fact, marriage requires the transformation of many social relationships. One cannot marry and behave like a single person with respect to time management, eating habits, and association with friends and relatives. However, the Bible zeroes in on the most basic of all relationships, that of the parent-child, to underscore the need of foundational changes that must take place in marriage.

> IT IS IMPORTANT FOR A NEWLYWED COUPLE TO REALIZE THAT IT IS IN THEIR INTEREST TO CHANGE THEIR RELATIONSHIP WITH THEIR PARENTS.

The process of marriage: cultivation of intimacy

While "leaving" is a decision that starts the marriage, "cleaving," or cultivating intimacy, is a process that a couple must work on throughout their marriage. The merging of the two lives into one inseparable unit is something that requires that the couple consciously choose to merge their use of time, their finances, and their aspirations and goals.

This is where prenuptial contracts are suspect for Christians. Besides the fact that divorce should not be contemplated as part of a Christian relationship, God expects His children to come together in an inseparable union. The means of cleaving are best discussed in the context of the product of biblical marriage—one flesh.

The product of biblical marriage: one flesh

The goal of leaving and cleaving is to become "one flesh," biblical terminology that connotes physical and sexual intimacy as well as oneness in soul and spirit.

The Bible is categorical that a true Christian, one who has accepted Jesus Christ as Lord and Saviour, should only marry another committed Christian (2 Corinthians 6:14), and that for a good reason. Spiritual oneness requires a common allegiance to Jesus Christ. The two must be indwelt by God's Holy Spirit. Spiritual oneness is then nurtured by praying and reading the Bible together, worshipping together, and serving together. Undergirded by unconditional love, these activities, over time, build both maturity and oneness between the couple.

Equally important is oneness in soul as the two draw near in will, intellect, feelings, and emotions. That requires transparent and honest communication, spending time together, and showing each other mutual respect and sensitivity. The hallmark of oneness in the soul is friendship between the couple.

Finally, intimacy is required in the physical realm whereby the husband and wife meet each other's physical, romantic, and sexual needs. Christian couples are encouraged to work on their sexual relationship and not defraud each other in matters of sex

(1 Corinthians 7:1-5). Because this is such a crucial area for couples, an entire book of the Bible, Song of Songs, is devoted to exulting sexual and romantic love within the marital relationship.

Duration: Christian marriage is for life

It would appear anachronistic to advocate lifelong marriage in an age when divorce, even among professing Christians, is so prevalent. But the will of God and the practice of men are often at variance. The Bible is unambiguous about the duration of marriage. Marriage is for life. "Therefore what God has joined together, let man not separate" (Matthew 19:6). The fact that we may fall below God's standards and need forgiveness does not alter the fact that God hates divorce (Malachi 2:14-16). The end of Christian marriage is the grave—"till death do us part!"

INTIMACY IS REQUIRED IN THE PHYSICAL REALM WHEREBY THE COUPLE MEETS EACH OTHER'S PHYSICAL, ROMANTIC, AND SEXUAL NEEDS.

Monogamous partnership: marriage is an exclusive relationship

Every direct teaching of Scripture on marriage implies that Christian marriage is to be between one man and one woman. God created male and female; a man is to leave his father and mother and cleave to his wife, not wives; what God has joined together no man is to separate. Yet polygamy is as old as the human race, with Lamech, the fifth generation after Adam, speaking of his wives (Genesis 4:23). Many Old Testament figures had more than one wife, especially the kings. Yet God's instruction as to how a king is to rule included the injunction not to take multiple wives (Deuteronomy 17:17). Thus, even a million wrongs in terms of the human practice of polygamy do not alter the divine will and ideal that marriage, as God intended it, is monogamous. Anyone who intends to marry as God has revealed in His Word must be committed to the exclusivity of marriage in a covenanted, monogamous relationship.

Marriage as God intended it comes with responsibilities for the spouses

The Bible provides guidelines that must govern the marital relationship. There are mutual responsibilities for both the husband and the wife implied in the mission of marriage. For example, both the man and the woman are to submit to each other's correction and discipline out of reverence for Christ (Ephesians 5:21); meet each other's sexual needs (1 Corinthians 7:3-5); honour and respect each other (Ephesians 5:33; 1 Peter 3:7); raise up godly children (Malachi 2:15); govern the earth, i.e., to fulfill the responsibility of working and serving in God's vineyard (Genesis 1:28); and help, support, befriend, and minister to each other (Genesis 2:18; Ephesians 5:28).

In addition to the mutual responsibilities of the couple, each spouse has unique responsibilities in his or her respective capacities as husband and wife. The wife, for example, is to submit to the husband's leadership (Ephesians 5:22); develop inward beauty (1 Peter 3:1-6); show *philia* (friendship) love to the husband (Titus 2:4); be a helpmate and do him good at all times (Proverbs 31:12); conduct herself in such a way as to earn her husband's confidence (Proverbs 31:11); and manage her household well (Proverbs 31:13-17).

THE CALLING OF GODLY HUSBANDS: THE ART OF LEADING ONE'S WIFE

Leadership required of Christian husbands is not a position but a function. Below are the functions of the biblical husband, a sort of "Ten Commandments of a Christian Husband." It may seem strange to discuss a husband leading his wife in the form of duties he has to perform. After all, you may say marriage is a loving relationship. However, love is not just a feeling or a set of emotions, but goodwill that always demonstrates itself in purposeful acts towards the well-being of the person loved. Jesus said, "If you love me, you will obey what I command" (John 14:15).

> THE BIBLICAL HUSBAND IS CALLED UPON TO INSPIRE, MOTIVATE, AND ENCOURAGE HIS SPOUSE TO STRIVE FOR EXCELLENCE.

Because men tend to be task-oriented, it is important that they understand love in terms of duties without denying the emotional and sentimental context. Love is an art to be learned, and the "Ten Commandments" of marital love for men form the basis of learning to love and lead one's wife meaningfully. Moreover, as these functions are performed, in all probability the wife will reciprocate as a partner.

A godly husband's duty is:

1. *To be a Christlike servant leader* (Ephesians 5:23). This is a calling to work with his wife to articulate mission, vision, goals, and strategies of the couple's relationship, not by issuing edicts, but through trustworthy character and service (servant leadership).

2. *To love his wife unconditionally* (Ephesians 5:25). The biblical husband is called upon to seek the welfare of his wife irrespective of her actions. In my opinion this is the greatest and most difficult duty of a Christian husband.

3. *To nurture his wife* (Ephesians 5:26-27). The parallel of this is seen in a gardener who tends a plant to maturity and fruitfulness through provision of water, fertilizers, and other stimuli needed for the growth of the plant. Contrary to what many husbands do, which is to accuse their wives of not meeting certain standards in the tradition of Adam's "the wife you gave me" excuse to God, the biblical husband is called upon to inspire, motivate, and encourage his spouse to strive for excellence. That may be in the areas of social, intellectual, and spiritual growth; or in the difficult tasks of keeping house and raising children.

4. *To live with her in knowledge* (1 Peter 3:7). Instead of the traditional generalization about women by men, husbands are to purposefully seek to know and understand their wives. Most men are simply ignorant about females. Thus they are either baffled, confused, or angered by women's behaviour; the complex chemical changes that take place in their bodies that affect their moods; and their responses to issues from the spiritual to the sexual. These are characteristics that do not make women inferior but different. Therefore, husbands are to take time to know their wives as women and as unique individuals.

> AS A LEADER, THE HUSBAND IS TO CONDUCT HIMSELF IN SUCH A WAY AS TO GIVE A GOOD NAME TO HIS WIFE AND FAMILY.

5. *To protect her.* Jesus spoke of a strong man guarding his house (Matthew 12:29). In ancient times the protection was physical. Today, many wives are crying for protection, not from physical harm but from insensitive people, from traditions that demean and abuse women, from bad in-laws, and sometimes even from their own children as they grow up. A godly husband builds spiritual, emotional, and physical protective walls around his wife that allow her to blossom, grow, and exercise her God-given gifts.

6. *To meet her needs.* Support in household chores has been found to be particularly important and ranked high in the emotional

needs of women in marriage. Another need that demands the special attention of the husband is her sexual needs. This is because men and women's sexual responses are different, with the result being that many wives' sexual needs are not being met.

My wife, Georgina, compares women to electric cookers and men to gas cookers in their sexual responses. In other words, they take different times to warm up. And yet the two are to cook the "food of sex" together and simultaneously. Many men do not appreciate the holistic view women take toward sex—their need for courteous treatment, romance, foreplay, and general intimacy in order for them to enjoy the sex act. It is the responsibility of a Christian husband to meet these sexual needs of his wife.

7. *To submit to his wife out of reverence for Christ.* Ephesians 5:21 asks Christian couples to submit to one another out of reverence for Christ. This is an often-neglected command for husbands who would rather jump over verse 21 to verse 22, where wives are called upon to submit to the husband's leadership. I believe that the essence of submission in Ephesians 5:21 for the husband involves listening to his wife's point of view and taking it into account in all decisions that affect the marriage and the family. It also involves accepting her correction in matters of wrongdoing, indiscretion, and sin; and above all, trusting her as a partner.

8. *To give her cause to be proud of him.* In almost every society, the name and image of the husband become the identity of the wife and the family, even where the adoption of the husband's surname in marriage is not the norm. As a leader, the husband is to conduct himself in such a way as to give a good name to his wife and family.

   I have sometimes wondered why Georgina, when I am fast asleep, will sit up in the night to wait for the news to come on television when she thinks I will be mentioned in it, especially when I have attended a function with her. I think she is concerned about the way the news reports on her husband. For her, "a good name is more desirable than great riches" (Proverbs 22:1).

9. *To bear her up before God.* The husband has a priestly function in the Christian home. That requires encouraging family and personal devotions. In addition, he bears his family up before the Lord in intercessory prayers. Like Job, he makes sure that they are sanctified in the Lord (Job 1:5). This is where Adam dropped the ball. In Eden, instead of yielding to Eve in sin, Adam should have stood firm and spiritually protected his wife. This is where Job again comes through as a model biblical husband. Instead of following his wife's advice to "curse God and die," he rebuked her, saying, "You are talking like a foolish woman. Shall we accept good from God, and not trouble?" (Job 2:9-10). And the couple lived to see better days.

Christian husbands are to bear their wives before God as Aaron wore the ephod before God. Instead, these days wives are likely to be the ones that build spiritual walls around the family as their husbands abandon their priestly responsibility.

10. *To praise her.* Every woman deserves to hear the immortal words of the husband of the noble woman: "Many women do noble things, but you surpass them all" (Proverbs 31:29). They should hear it in private and before the children, in-laws, and friends. All women have need for admiration and acknowledgement of their beauty and service. And it is not mere flattery, for the worth of a wife is more than pearls. I believe the extraordinary intelligence, diligence, wisdom, hard work, and social sensitivity of the noble woman of Proverbs 31 was so evident partly because her husband and family praised her for her surpassing worth, her beauty, and her godliness. She was encouraged to strive for excellence. Moreover, they gave her the rewards she had earned, not only at home, but by letting "her works bring her praise at the city gate" (Proverbs 31:31).

I am fully convinced that if Christian husbands undertake the above functions, they will create a unique atmosphere within which they will lead the marriage partnership in vision setting, undertaking the mission of marriage, dealing with inevitable problems, and raising future leaders out of their children. If that is not leading one's wife, I know not of other better means.

MARITAL FLASH POINTS AND ENEMIES

One of the functions of a leader is making difficult decisions and solving big problems. It does not mean the leader thereby becomes all-knowing. In fact, in the business world, often the chief executive may not have a clue to the technical solutions to most of the major problems. But it remains his responsibility to find those who can help to resolve the difficulty. Good leaders work with their team and foster group decisions. Nevertheless, the buck stops with the leader. A good leader, therefore, must anticipate problems, seek solutions, and make decisions.

. GOOD LEADERS WORK WITH THEIR TEAM AND FOSTER GROUP DECISIONS. NEVERTHELESS, THE BUCK STOPS WITH THE LEADER. A GOOD LEADER, THEREFORE, MUST ANTICIPATE PROBLEMS, SEEK SOLUTIONS, AND MAKE DECISIONS.

While predicting all the problems in human relations is impossible, in marriage five areas have generated most marital conflicts. My wife and I call them the marital flash points. They are communication, sex, money, children, and in-laws.

I will not even attempt to elaborate on these marital flash points, as each would require a whole chapter or even a book on its own. Fortunately, there are many good Christian books on the market, including three we have written, on communication, parenting, and personal finances (see list of references). It will suffice to say that it is a leadership responsibility of the husband to lead his wife in ensuring that these marital flash points are anticipated and managed well.

In addition to providing leadership to manage the marital flash points, effective male leadership requires dealing with three enemies of Christian marriage, namely, self, tradition, and Satan.

In his leadership role, the husband must resist self-centredness and selfishness, the tendency to resort to cultural practices, and the norms of the world instead of the teaching of God's Word. Neither must he allow Satan to undermine the marriage as a Christ-centred, God-honouring relationship.

REAL MEN OR WIMPS?

When men are called upon to provide Christlike servant leadership to their wives, some men feel that their wives will take advantage of them. This is particularly so in traditional societies, such as one finds in developing countries. In other words, there is genuine fear that a shift from the traditional, dominant husband-father figure will undermine male authority, respect, and the overall leadership of the husband.

I agree that some women may take advantage of their husbands, to the detriment of both spouses. After all, we live in a fallen, sin-sick world, and even when we are saved by grace we still struggle with our old nature. But the good news is that God's ways

IT IS IN
THE CONSTITUTION
OF WOMEN TO RESPOND
TO EFFECTIVE LOVING
SERVANT LEADERSHIP WITH
SUBMISSION AND LOVE.

are for our good and are perfect, and that servant leadership is a win-win proposition for both the husband and his wife. I have five reasons for this confidence:

First, it is in the constitution of women to respond to effective loving servant leadership with submission and love.

Second, her real needs for affection, conversation, trust, comfort and cuddling, family commitment, and admiration demand male leadership.

Third, the performance of the male leadership role will help women fulfill their own roles as wives and mothers.

Fourth, it seems that loving and serving come more naturally to women than men. Thus, the biblical role of men addresses, in part, male weaknesses.

Fifth, women and indeed men love to be led by servant leaders.

It is the Christian husband's privilege to love and nurture his wife, and in doing so he provides a strong foundation for the raising of children. We now turn to the crucial role that fathers fill in the lives of their children.

QUESTIONS:

1. Why is it important that the man be the leader of the wife? What is required of him in that role?

2. What form should that leadership take?

3. What are some of the purposes of a Christian marriage?

4. Why is it important for a married couple to have the proper relationship with in-laws?

CHAPTER NINE

LEADING ONE'S CHILDREN

If *partnership* is the closest word from the corporate world to describe the art of leading one's wife, mentoring lies at the heart of leading one's children. Fatherhood is probably the most challenging of all the jobs facing a Christian man—and probably the most joyful. This is because it entails the raising of eternal souls and impacting generations yet unborn. I will discuss parenting from the point of view of the father, but being that it's a shared responsibility between the spouses, much of the contents apply equally to the mother.[1]

PARENTING: A NOBLE CALLING

Of all the names and attributes of God, none is as comforting and meaningful to people, especially Christians, as that of Father. In this title, all the promises of God and His attributes of love, providence, and care are encapsulated. Moreover, in the love of God, we see the redemption that Jesus Christ provides through His shed blood and consequent reconciliation between sinful man and a Holy God. Through Jesus' work of redemption, God has granted us the highest status in heaven—sonship.

It is in the context of the fatherhood of God that we are called to be parents. In that regard, there are certain key parental roles and responsibilities set forth in the Bible.

In the preceding chapter, we noted that husbands owe their wives the duty of a "good name." That applies even more to their role as parents. A name is one of the most important legacies anyone could give to their children. "The son of . . ." is a father's number one legacy to his children. "A good name is more desirable than great riches [material legacy]; to be esteemed is better than silver or gold" (Proverbs 22:1).

Again, 1 Timothy 3:1-7, which talks about an overseer or elder or bishop, has been narrowly applied to leaders within the church as an institution, to the neglect of the church in the home. Be that as it may, in its broader context, Paul's portrait of the elder is the male parallel of the noble woman in Proverbs 31:10-31. It is a description of a godly husband and father who leaves the legacy of a good name as a model for his children.

Another key parental role is to provide protection for the children. Jesus, speaking of Jerusalem's refusal to embrace His love and salvation, said, "How often I have longed to gather your children together, as a hen gathers her chicks under her wings" (Matthew 23:37). This picture often came to mind when I tucked my children in at night. As someone brought up in the countryside where fowls ranged freely, I often saw a hen gather her chicks with lightning speed under her wings because she had seen a hawk aiming at them. Because the hen was heavier in weight, the hawk would not be able to lift her, and hence her chicks were protected.

Jesus depicted a father as a strong man who, protecting his house, guards it against thieves (Luke 11:21). These days the protection is likely to be more ethical, moral, and spiritual than physical, even though one must not underestimate the physical harm children may be exposed to from school bullies, predators, and drug peddlers.

A third biblical function of a father, and parents in general, is to provide the material needs of their children. The Bible says it is the responsibility of parents to provide the needs of their children and not vice versa (2 Corinthians 12:14). The writer of Proverbs adds that "a good man leaves an inheritance for his children's children" (13:22).

Central to the responsibilities of a godly man is the necessity to instruct his children in the training and instruction of the Lord (Ephesians 6:4). The Lord made it plain to Abraham, and to every father, the purpose of his calling as follows:

For I have chosen him, so that he will direct his children and his household after him to keep the way of the Lord by doing what is right and just, so that the LORD will bring about for Abraham what he has promised him. (Genesis 18:19)

In Deuteronomy 6:4-9 fathers are called upon to love the Lord wholly and to pass this practice on to their children. This they should do by training or bringing them up to distinguish between good and evil. Training children goes beyond verbal instructions. Fathers should be good role models and encourage and discipline their children to achieve the same. Training children, therefore, constitutes the fourth responsibility of fathers.

Even though one can subsume it under training, discipline is so important that I should mention it as a separate responsibility of a father. One of the major contributions of Dr. James Dobson, the founder of Focus of the Family, is on this subject of discipline, beginning with his seminal book, *Dare to Discipline,* and many others that have followed. The balance between love and discipline is the mark of an effective father.

It is worth reiterating that a father has a responsibility to pray and bear his family up daily as Job did before God (Job 1:5). As we battle for the souls of our family members, we should be conscious that we are not fighting against flesh and blood but against heavenly hosts of wickedness (Ephesians 6:12). "With this in mind, be alert and always keep on praying for all the saints" (Ephesians 6:18). There is another reason why we must pray for our children. We hold them in trust for God and, as such, must account to Him who gives them to us. In bringing them before God, we acknowledge that we are trustees only.

Finally, we owe our children unconditional love. One of the things that distinguished Jesus from others was that He had no doubt of His Father's love. God the Father made that point at an appropriate time. He affirmed, "This is my Son, whom I love; with him I am well pleased" (Matthew 3:17). In the parable of the prodigal son, Jesus demonstrated the unconditional love of a father who waited in love to receive his son back home, even after he had wasted his inheritance (Luke 15:11-32).

> TRAINING CHILDREN GOES BEYOND VERBAL INSTRUCTIONS. FATHERS SHOULD BE GOOD ROLE MODELS AND ENCOURAGE AND DISCIPLINE THEIR CHILDREN TO ACHIEVE THE SAME.

The foregoing responsibilities of parents, and especially of fathers— (i) to give a good name to their children; (ii) to protect them; (iii) to provide for their physical needs; (iv) to instruct and train them; (v) to discipline them; (vi) to pray for them, and (vii) to love them unconditionally—should form the basis of leading our children amidst the challenges in today's increasingly bad environment, raising the Josephs and Daniels of our day.

RAISING GOOD KIDS IN A BAD WORLD

Fathers must be aware of their divine responsibilities toward their children. They must also take into account the context in which they are to exercise their fatherhood, that is, the world we live in. And that world is not friendly toward raising godly kids. An hour in front of the TV screen or a glance through a typical newspaper is alarming enough. We live in a world that is sliding downhill morally and socially:

CHRISTIAN PARENTS ARE NOT TO THROW IN THE TOWEL, BLAME TODAY'S GENERATION, OR THINK THAT OUR PARENTS HAD IT EASIER. EVERY GENERATION IS RESPONSIBLE FOR RAISING THE DANIELS OF THE NEXT GENERATION.

• God is being crossed out in our language, in our schools, and at work. We are experiencing a loss of God consciousness.

• We are led to believe that man lives by bread alone, and the spiritual is being ridiculed as a fairy tale. Materialism abounds.

• Relative and situational morality with no absolutes is the norm rather than the exception.

• Globalisation of immorality is the order of the day thanks to cable and global TV networks.

• Pornography is easily accessible on the Internet. Many people, especially men, have fallen prey to this form of "entertainment."

• Breakdown of families and values is seen everywhere.

• Violence in the form of demonic books, music, and films desensitises young people from the effects of direct exposure to Satan and his demons.

• Safe neighbourhoods are shrinking, with alcohol and drug abuse on the increase.

- This is an age of tyranny of the "expert," where an ungodly social worker, educated for three years, is likely to be recognized as more of an authority on your child than the people who follow godly and time-tested principles of raising kids.

Yet Christian parents are not to throw in the towel, blame today's generation, or think that our parents had it easier. Every generation is responsible for raising the Daniels of the next generation.

The encouraging news is that raising good kids in this bad world is possible. Given the right attitude, knowledge, and skills, we can lead our families in the right way with the help of God. There are more tools and resources for parenting today than ever before. The Bible, God's unchanging rule of life, is still ours to follow. We have resources of godly experts and other specialists readily available to us. Churches often provide seminars or small groups that focus on parenting. More than anything else, God is our helper. Remember that "Jesus Christ is the same yesterday and today and forever" (Hebrews 13:8).

EQUIPPING YOURSELF FOR THE TASK OF LEADING YOUR CHILDREN

As we have previously discussed, effective parents will remember several important elements when raising their children: The father must be a model, mentor, and minister to his children. Furthermore, the best thing a man can do for his children is to love their mother. And the home should be a place where Jesus is worshipped as Lord, where a genuine love prevails, where the family works together and learns social relationships, and where godly authority is respected.

IN LEADING ONE'S CHILDREN EFFECTIVELY, A FATHER MUST HAVE A POSITIVE ATTITUDE AND HIGH REGARD FOR THE JOB OF RAISING CHILDREN.

The following issues are additional to the art of raising godly kids. *Adopt a positive attitude to parenting.* Nothing illustrates the right attitude as much as a story by Gordon MacDonald in his book *The Effective Father.* He tells the story of two bricklayers who were working on a church building. One described himself as "a builder of a great cathedral," while the other saw himself as an underpaid bricklayer. Both did the same job, but their attitudes in words and deed were worlds apart, and so I presume was their satisfaction.

In leading one's children effectively, a father must have a positive attitude and high regard for the job of raising children. The child should not take second or third place after a vocation, church duties, or recreation. Children are a heritage from the Lord. You could say that godly parenting can be likened to building great cathedrals in which He is honoured and worshipped. Paul summed it up this way: "We proclaim him, admonishing and teaching everyone with all wisdom, so that we may present everyone perfect [mature] in Christ" (Colossians 1:28). Our goal, then, is to raise our children "mature in Christ."

Set right goals as a leader of your children. Often fathers have hidden aspirations for their children to be doctors, engineers, or some other professional. That usually reflects their own profession or their unfulfilled aspirations or what they perceive as a high-income profession. For example, as a child, I wanted to be an engineer but ended up as an economist. The temptation is to make engineers of my children.

I think as Christian fathers, our principal goal must be to raise mature Christians who fulfill their God-given destiny. When our daughter Priscilla, a straight-A science student, decided to be a teacher rather than a doctor or dentist as I would have preferred, I was still delighted that she chose to use her gifts in raising young lives. Here, as in all areas of our lives, Jesus is our model. In Luke 2:52 we read, "And Jesus grew in wisdom and stature, and in favour with God and men." I think the vision and goal of Christian fathers should be that their children achieve physical, intellectual, spiritual, and social growth and become useful tools in God's hands.

Acquire basic knowledge and skills of parenting. Few people start parenting as experts. In that regard, there is no virtue in ignorance or blind reliance on custom and tradition. The Bible says, "My people are destroyed from lack of knowledge" (Hosea 4:6). Christian parents must acquaint themselves with Scripture's rich teaching on parenting, especially in the book of Proverbs. Then there are excellent books on parenting by godly men and women. In our own family, Georgina and I have had cause to thank God over and over again for the writings of saints, such as Larry Christensen's *The Christian Family,* James Dobson's *Dare to Discipline,* and Chuck Swindoll's *Hand Me Another Brick.*

For our family, books such as *Leading Little Ones to God* by M. M. Schoolland and P. Stout and the various writings of Dr. Kenneth Taylor of *The Living Bible* fame, as well as publications of the Scripture Union, have been Godsent to us. As the kids grew up, we introduced them to Oswald Chambers' *My Utmost for His Highest* and the equally exceptional writing of E. Stanley Jones in *Abundant Living.* Both were written in the first half of the 20th century, and yet they are as contemporary as today's publications. We also used Ladybird Books for the teaching of reading. We have found that whenever we had need or discovered our ignorance, help was around.

THE FATHER IN HIS LEADERSHIP MUST DO TWO THINGS. HE MUST BUILD A TEAM WITH HIS WIFE TO RAISE GODLY CHILDREN. THE SECOND IS TO LOVE THEIR MOTHER.

God is our ally in raising good kids in a bad world. But on earth, he does not require us to raise our children on Robinson Crusoe's island. He has given us human, institutional, and material resources for our use. When I talk about praying and interceding for our children and going through God's Word, I have in mind availing ourselves of God's spiritual resources.

In that regard, I found that my wife is God's greatest resource for me in leading my family. A godly wife is indeed a helpmate. Leading your children is not ordinarily meant to be a single-parent job. While the death of a spouse does every now and then lead to single parenthood, the current spate of premarital pregnancies, divorce, and the resulting phenomenon of so many single parents was not anticipated in Scripture, where the church was encouraged to take care of widows and orphans. Single parents require encouragement and support, but a two-parent family is the norm in Scripture. The father in his leadership must do two things. He must build a team with his wife to raise godly children. It's a partnership. The second, let me repeat, is that by far the most important gift that any father can give to his children is to love their mother. Otherwise, nothing a father does is likely to compensate for the psychological damage to his children. "Leading your wife" is therefore a prerequisite for the effective leadership of children.

I enjoy parenting, but I find it also a most challenging and most humbling experience. One cannot predict what lies ahead. Georgina and I were not prepared for what lay ahead when we married. We had the joy of seeing our firstborn, Stephen, graduate at 23 with two degrees, a B.Sc. (Civil Engineering) and B.A. (Commerce). His photograph adorns our family room as the first of many graduation photographs. But within weeks of his graduation he was struck down with a serious illness, which he is still struggling with after three years. In all that, the unchanging factor was the love of God in Jesus. We now appreciate parents who have to live with mentally or physically challenged children.

PARENTING INVOLVES EQUIPPING THE CHILD

We as parents have the responsibility of launching our children into adulthood with the skills needed to be successful, and we do so in several ways:

ONE OF THE GREATEST INJUSTICES WE CAN DO TO OUR CHILDREN IS TO FORCE ON THEM A VISION AGAINST THEIR BENT.

Give the child a vision. In raising kids, as in growing other leaders, a major factor in success is giving the child a vision. It is not enough to just have one's own goals, important as that may be. The more important thing is giving or rather encouraging and guiding the child to have a vision. One of the reasons many parents have a tough time with their teenage children is this lack of vision early in their lives.

Our daughter Eunice is one of those rare creatures who, as early as 4, knew what she wanted to be: a physician. Parenting all our four children was a delight, but parenting Eunice was almost effortless. She was focused, organized, and determined. At age 17 she applied to 17 universities, and in all cases her choice was medicine, medicine, and medicine. Her parents, who are not that focused themselves, tried to encourage her to broaden her choice, but she was undeterred. She illustrates what can happen when a child has a vision. (We later realized that all the family physicians Eunice had encountered were women. She had formed the view that being a physician was a woman's job. One day she and her younger sister burst into laughter when their older brother suggested he might be a doctor. The young girls were surprised that a man could contemplate studying medicine.)

Giving a child a vision, however, is not as easy as it sounds. This is because parents sometimes seek to live their own unfulfilled aspirations through their children. A teenager once confided, "All I want to study is French, but my parents insist that I study medicine. I will do it, provided it is in French." One of the greatest injustices we can do to our children is to force on them a vision against their bent. We should challenge our children to explore their interests but not try to impose our vision on them, especially in the choice of their careers. How can we do this?

- Encourage them to be holistic, that is, not to focus unduly on the academic and the professional but on Christian maturity. Let them have a vision as servants of the Lord with all other things—professions, earnings, marriage, etc.— being subordinated to that.

- Encourage them to be able to lead and manage their lives. The goal of parenting should be to groom mature adults who will ultimately be independent of the parents.

- Train them to learn how to set spiritual, intellectual, social, financial, and other goals and strive for excellence.

- Inculcate in them the disciplines and habits of godly people.

Develop the child's positive self-image. At school, in the marketplace, in the real world, a child is likely to meet sexual, racial, and other forms of discrimination. As a result, sometimes one comes across a most beautiful, intelligent child and, by all standards, a winner who because of a cruel word from a teacher, a colleague, or due to one unfortunate incident or other, feels unloved, useless, and unattractive. That person is pushed into having low self-esteem. Though there is a thin line between pride and a positive self-image, that line must be drawn and a positive image developed in your child. How critical is this parenting responsibility! Your encouragement and love can counteract the negative messages your child may be hearing outside the home.

However, the basis of our positive self-image as Christians should not be our race, or social status, wealth, or education, but in the fact that we are of intrinsic value because God made us in His image and sent Jesus to die for us. The Bible says, "Let him who boasts boast about this: that he understands and knows [the Lord]" (Jeremiah 9:24).

Maintain effective communication. One of the effective ways to make your child feel significant is through your communication with him or her. At the root of most parent-child problems is ineffective communication. This is an area where many parents have been discouraged at one time or another.

Effective communication with your children demands that the parents make some adjustments in schedule to spend time with them, listen actively to them, and set an example in positive communication that builds one up (see Ephesians 4:29). It includes seeking to understand their world—emotions, disappointments, pressures—without being quick to make judgments.

Your children must learn the general principles of effective communication: appreciation, managing one's emotions, listening effectively, conflict resolution, demonstration of total love, and the use of verbal and nonverbal communication.

Make the child feel unconditionally loved. Unfortunately, many fathers think that all they need to do is pay school fees, provide physical necessities, and occasionally buy ice cream. In our booklet titled *How to Raise Good Kids in a Bad World,* we list eight ways in which to show the child unconditional love:

- The parents must themselves experience unconditional love in Christ and express gratitude for that.

- The kids will learn from your experience of the love of Christ. It is contagious.

- Exert the right parental authority. Children require a sense of authority and the setting of limits to feel secure and loved.

- Share times and activities with them from their point of view. They want to see you at the sideline when they play competitive games; be at Parent-Teacher Association meetings; inconvenience yourself occasionally to answer their demands.

- Give affirmation and warmth, and touch them.

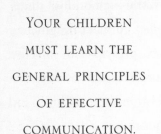

YOUR CHILDREN MUST LEARN THE GENERAL PRINCIPLES OF EFFECTIVE COMMUNICATION.

- Select appropriate gifts, especially ones that show them you understand their age, without condoning excesses.

- Anticipate their needs and meet them before they ask you.

- Be available for their special occasions whenever possible and just not at your convenience.

Unconditional love is not a philosophy to children. It must be experienced. The bottom line is that they must know they are accepted unconditionally, even when they are being disciplined.

Talk about discipline. The Preacher said, "Discipline your son, and he will give you peace; he will bring delight to your soul" (Proverbs 29:17). In fact, failure to discipline your child is tantamount to being an accomplice in his death (Proverbs 19:18). While it is the responsibility of parents to discipline their children, it must be done always from the child's point of view. Those who have not read Dr. James Dobson's books on disciplining children must look for them now. In them we learn that your discipline must be goal directed and for the good of the child; must start early in their lives; must balance discipline with love; and must be perceived by the child as just, fair, reasonable, and appropriate in relation to the offence. Couples must discuss styles of discipline and ensure they do not send conflicting signals.

Train up the child. A verse in the Bible that seems to sum up all that leading our children entails is Proverbs 22:6: "Train a child in the way he should go, and when he is old he will not turn from it." Fathers are to instruct their children in the ways of the Lord, developing their minds, building their decision-making capacity, teaching them how to cultivate friendships and handle money, and generally how to live. That is not the job of the school. It is important to train them according to their age, position in the family, and temperaments. Training must be consistent and backed by prayer and discipline. We advise parents to train their children in anticipation of the next stage of life. For example, the time to equip a child for the teenage years is in the pre-teen years.

Training must be backed by example. Parents must walk their talk. If kids are to read the Bible, they must see Daddy do so; if they are not to swear, father must not; if they are to be truthful and honest, parents must not cheat on their tax returns.

Encourage habit formation. Last but not the least, let me share a principle very dear to my heart: habit formation. If one is successful in parenting, the result should be the creation of an independent, balanced, and mature adult out of your child. In other words, while giving them roots you must develop their wings to fly. You want them to develop integrity and principle-centred Christian living first and foremost. Also important is the formation of good habits to anchor the lessons of life. These would include reading God's Word each day, exercising, and habits of personal hygiene. These must be part of the upbringing of our children, and Daddy must show the way.

Since leadership is an art, it is unwise to be too prescriptive. We therefore conclude this chapter by inviting fathers to ponder the roles they play in their children's lives.

To your children there is no substitute for a father. And leading one's family is a father's job. The father is a model, lover, leader, teacher, judge, guardian, and provider for his children.

QUESTIONS:

1. How does God model the ideal father?

2. What is a central responsibility of a godly father?

3. What role should custom and traditions play in raising children?

4. What is the greatest challenge you've faced as a parent? The most humbling moment? The funniest incident?

CHAPTER TEN

LEADING ONE'S FAMILY WITH INTEGRITY

I n this final chapter of the book, I want to address the living reality that leadership can be both functional and dysfunctional. The difference involves integrity and credibility.

Leadership always impacts others because the essence of leadership is influencing others. I have demonstrated in the preceding chapters how a leader can and usually does influence, simultaneously, himself, his family, and colleagues. This he does by inspiring and motivating others to realise their full potential. In fact, the greater impact of the leader is multiplied, not through what he does directly, but through others.

It is this power of leaders to catalyse others—call it inspiration, motivation, empowerment, or "encouraging the heart," to use the phraseology of J. M. Kouzes and B. Z. Posner in their book of the same name[1]—that makes leadership such a powerful agent.

Once you adopt a leadership lifestyle, hundreds, even thousands of people are impacted by you just being yourself.

In August 2003 I felt humbled but at the same time learned the impact of leadership. It was a joyful sight and, in the end, an extremely embarrassing one when I spoke to a group of about 500 young people on "Breaking Barriers to Leadership." It was joyful because I could see from their faces the desire to make their lives count. The embarrassing part came when my wife and I started to leave the hall. Not only did they give us a standing ovation, but they formed a guard of honour for us, clapping until we entered our car and drove off. That day I knew that we were called to inspire others, especially the youth, to be leaders.

> LEADERSHIP ALWAYS IMPACTS OTHERS BECAUSE THE ESSENCE OF LEADERSHIP IS INFLUENCING OTHERS.

DYSFUNCTIONAL LEADERSHIP

But leadership is a double-edged sword. Leadership can be functional or tragically dysfunctional. How many homes have been devastated because a father has either abandoned his responsibility totally or has become egotistic and selfish? Increasingly, fatherlessness has become so common that it is only by God's grace that children survive the result. The bane of many young brides is

that after marriage they become constrained by lack of good hus-
bandly leadership. They are left to grope in the dark, without mission or vision. These women are often left alone to lead their homes.

A visitor from Australia to our home in Accra asked during a
leadership discussion, "What makes the difference between functional
and dysfunctional leadership?" My off-the-cuff response, which on
reflection I am convinced is the truth, was the heart. The Bible says
that ordinarily we are all prone to abuse the privilege of having an
influence over others, which leadership is. In biblical language,
Jeremiah puts it this way: "The heart is deceitful above all things" and
adds that only the Lord understands it (Jeremiah 17:9-10).

Many of us, even Christians, underestimate our power to do
evil even though we have been saved by grace. The only ways we
will not become dysfunctional are:

- *To be controlled by the Holy Spirit of God.* The Spirit will
  convict us of the sins of righteousness and of judgment.
  The leader may not be told by his followers that he is
  wrong, even if they see he is. But God's Spirit in us will. As
  we learn to listen to the voice of God, we are saved from the
  abuse of power. The Spirit of God builds in us character
  (Galatians 5:22-24).

- *To be guided in our conduct by the Word of God.* "Your word is
  a lamp to my feet and a light for my path" (Psalm 119:105).

- *By avoiding concentrating power in yourself.* Even when you are
  a pioneer, it pays to form a team and create an accountability group. As historian Lord Acton said, "Power corrupts,

and absolute power corrupts absolutely." That is why at home God gives us our spouses as partners; at work, management teams; and at the corporate level, a board of directors.

- *At all times strive to be a person of integrity.*

LEADING WITH INTEGRITY

"Integrity has to do with consistency between what is inside a person and what is outside; between belief and behaviour; our words and our ways, our attitudes and our actions, our values and our practice. Integrity is the direct opposite of hypocrisy—it is the quality that people want most to see in a leader."[2] A study of American managers found that they most valued honesty and integrity in their leaders.[3] To the study's authors, integrity breeds *credibility.* People want to follow people who are trustworthy and are "principle-centred," to borrow the words of Stephen Covey.[4]

PEOPLE OFTEN LACK INTEGRITY BECAUSE THEY ARE CONCERNED ONLY WITH PUBLIC BEHAVIOUR AND THUS VIOLATE THEIR OWN ETHICS.

People often lack integrity because they are concerned only with public behaviour and thus violate their own ethics. This is what the Pharisees of Jesus' day did (Matthew 6:1-24). It does not mean a man of integrity does nothing wrong. But even if he violates his sense of integrity, he never glosses over it, makes excuses, or takes it lightly. Rather, he admits it, apologises for it, and moves on. Followers don't look for angelic leaders, but honest men and women, people of integrity who are nevertheless human and fallible.

It is insightful to know that God describes the biblical King David as a man of integrity (1 Kings 9:4). Though David committed adultery, he was genuinely repentant. His sin broke his heart (Psalms 32, 40, and 51).

FOUNDATIONS FOR CREDIBLE LEADERS OF INTEGRITY

To me, there are three elements that make for effective leadership. They may be called the three Cs of legacy-building leadership in the home. They are character, competence, and care (see Figure 10.1).

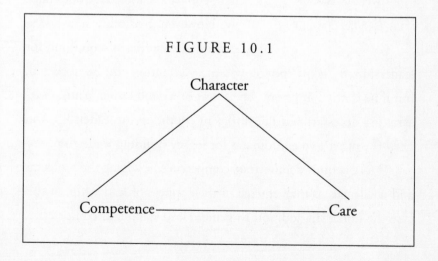

FIGURE 10.1

Character

Competence ——————————— Care

LEGACY-BUILDING LEADERSHIP

Credibility in leadership comes out of character, competence, and care for followers. Because of the importance of credibility in the enduring leadership of the servant leader, I want to expand briefly on what I mean by character, competence, and care.

It is impossible to be an effective leader in your home without being a man of character. By character, I am talking of being a person of integrity and trustworthiness, a person of transparent honesty, being humble, self-disciplined, God-fearing, and principle centred. Dependable character is a nonnegotiable element in godly leadership. In short, you have to be credible. That is hard in the home because the last people to be fooled are one's family. However, credibility is a necessary but not sufficient condition for leadership. A "good" person will draw attention and be respected, but if he is not competent, he cannot be a good leader. Thus, character is a necessary but not sufficient condition for leadership. You need the other two coordinates for legacy-building leadership.

. A "GOOD" PERSON WILL DRAW ATTENTION AND BE RESPECTED, BUT IF HE IS NOT COMPETENT, HE CANNOT BE A GOOD LEADER.

Leaders must demonstrate competence in solving the problems and challenges as they emerge in their sphere of leadership, in this case the home. In addition to generic leadership and competence, the leader in the home has to acquire the specific skills to motivate and inspire his wife and lead his children. For example, even though I was a trained teacher, I had to learn how to teach a toddler to be interested in books. Similarly, not coming from a Christian home, I had to learn about leading little ones to God.

As leadership is an art of influencing others, people want to feel care and empathy in their leaders. Leaders empower, motivate, and inspire others to bring the best out of them and make them feel valuable. A major distinction between leaders and managers is that the former major on inspiring and motivating followers, whereas the latter focus on systems and controls. This is particularly so in the family, when your spouse or children are less likely to listen to your lectures on leadership or management. They want to feel loved and cared for. This is where servant leaders win, hands down. Servant leaders major on serving others. Like all transformational leaders, they combine character with a high degree of competence and skills. Servant leaders aim first and foremost at the betterment of their followers.

AREAS OF INTEGRITY IN PRACTICE

Integrity is not a private or philosophical matter for the leader. Followers want to see and feel credibility. Integrity is practical and must be reflected in each of the major areas of life, including our worldview, family life, our finances, and our work. I have provided the table on page 181 to help readers identify where they stand with regard to integrity in their personal lives. It may be one of the most important exercises you will do. It will help you identify your ethical stands, your self-assessment of how well you are doing, and plans for improvement.

INTEGRITY IS NOT
A PRIVATE OR
PHILOSOPHICAL MATTER
FOR THE LEADER.
FOLLOWERS WANT
TO SEE AND
FEEL CREDIBILITY.

INTERPRETATION

An integrity quotient below 80 means you have a serious problem with integrity; 80 and above indicates you are doing well—provided your values are right. Regardless of your integrity quotient, aim to improve to 100 percent by giving greater attention to your lowest ratings in column (3). Then consider comparing your values to the standards in the Bible, such as the Ten Commandments or the Sermon on the Mount.

MODEL LEADERS OF INTEGRITY IN THE BIBLE

One of the best ways to learn integrity is to study men and women who lived under stressful situations. The Bible has recorded great examples for us, and I find that one of the most powerful ways to work on your integrity is to study these leaders. In them you meet people of unblemished integrity as well as leaders who dropped

TABLE 10.1
INTEGRITY ANALYSIS TABLE

(1) AREA OF LIFE	(2) LIST THREE CORE VALUES OF YOURS IN THE LIGHT OF THE BIBLE	(3) ON A SCALE OF 1 (LOWEST) TO 5 (HIGHEST), GRADE HOW YOU WOULD RATE YOURSELF ACCORDING TO YOUR ETHICAL STANDARD	(4) LIST THE SINGLE MOST IMPORTANT ACTION YOU WILL TAKE TO IMPROVE YOUR INTEGRITY TO INCREASE YOUR SCORES IN (3)
1. Spiritual life	1. (i) (ii) (iii)		
2. Intellectual life	2. (i) (ii) (iii)		
3. Social life	3. (i) (ii) (iii)		
4. Financial life	4. (i) (ii) (iii)		
5. Marital life	5. (i) (ii) (iii)		
6. Family Life (Relations with children)	6. (i) (ii) (iii)		
7. Physical life (health)	7. (i) (ii) (iii)		
8. Professional Life (Vocational)	8. (i) (ii) (iii)		
9. Other (Specify)	9. (i) (ii) (iii)		
Total of Column (3)			

Framework for Scoring

A) Total of column 3 =_____

B) Your total in A divided by 27 =_____

C) Your integrity quotient is your answer in B divided by 5, times 100 (B/5 x 100)

Write your integrity quotient here:_____

the ball of integrity. I provide examples of both below to guide your personal study in the Bible:

Men and women of integrity include:
- Joseph (Genesis 39)

- Samuel (1 Samuel 12:1-5)

- Daniel and friends (Daniel 1–6)

- Esther (Esther 4)

- Paul (1 Corinthians 9)

Examples of lack of integrity:
- Achan (Joshua 7)

- Judah (Genesis 38)

- Gehazi (2 Kings 5)

- Hezekiah (2 Chronicles 32:14, 26, 31)

- Ananias and Sapphira (Acts 5:1-11)

HOW TO BECOME
A PERSON OF INTEGRITY

Hard as it is to teach integrity to grown-ups, I list below eight ideas that may help people take integrity seriously. This assumes that one knows Jesus Christ as Lord and Saviour.

STEP 1: *Personal identity.* "Who am I?" The Akans of Ghana say, "Animguase? mfata kani ba," i.e., "Disgrace does not befit an Akan."

If so, how about a child of God? Self-respect for who you are is the beginning of a life of integrity. This is where you have to confront yourself to see whether you have truly repented and trusted Jesus as Lord and Saviour. If we are true Christians, then the Bible says we are ambassadors of Christ (2 Corinthians 5:20). In other words, God calls those who have trusted Jesus to be His ambassadors. Being an ambassador means you have to behave in a manner consistent with being a diplomat. In the same way integrity is required of us as children of God, husbands, and fathers. The other day I had to tell a member of my family, "You are an Adei," in response to why certain things cannot be done. How much more so for a child of God and "an ambassador of Christ"!

STEP 2: *Purpose and beliefs.* All people—Christians, Muslims, members of other faiths, unbelievers—have belief systems that affect their attitude toward sex, money, lying, and even murder. What you believe is important to your sense of integrity. If your ethics are wrong, even if you exercise integrity, the consequence will remain wrong. Therefore, clarify your purpose in life (Ecclesiastes 12:13) and your belief system. The Ten Commandments and the Sermon on the Mount have no equivalents on earth or in any other religion. Accepting these as rules of life is foundational to being a man of integrity.

STEP 3: *Articulation of values.* Honesty, transparency, and principle centredness are values one learns. Christian values must be Bible based rather than driven by our tradition or culture or the society one lives in. A man of integrity has core values he lives by.

STEP 4: *Prior reflection on core ethical challenges.* One of the greatest aids to a life of integrity is to think prayerfully through challenges in the core areas of your life—*before* they hit you. For example, as a U.N. economic adviser who had to spend a lot of the time sleeping in hotels, I knew that I faced sexual temptations. A CEO faces the tendency to abuse power and use official office for private gain. Anticipating these helps to deal with such a situation when it arises. In that regard, the areas I will be called upon to exercise integrity relate to the same areas that formed the basis of our personal strategic plan, such as spiritual life, marriage, parenting, finances, and friendship. No one ever gets tempted in areas he has nothing to do with. I have never been tempted as a politician or a clergyman because I have not been one.

WHAT YOU BELIEVE IS IMPORTANT TO YOUR SENSE OF INTEGRITY. IF YOUR ETHICS ARE WRONG, EVEN IF YOU EXERCISE INTEGRITY, THE CONSEQUENCE WILL REMAIN WRONG.

STEP 5: *Develop and/or join a formal or informal accountability group.* Men tend to do well when they share things within a group. The Promise Keepers are positively impacting men because they get men into groups and hold each other accountable, formally and informally. As leader of your family, you will benefit from having an accountability group. In fact, your spouse and children are your best allies in being a man of integrity. But you may have other friends from church and work as part of the group, provided they share similar convictions.

STEP 6: *Grow in the Lord.* Some people think growing in Christian maturity requires a magic wand. In reality the key is a consistent walk with Jesus. You do so by making progress in the following areas:

- Be sure you are born again or have rededicated your life to Jesus (John 3:1-5, 16).

- Undertake a daily search through Scripture and let its standards inform your living (Joshua 1:8-9; Psalm 119:105).

- Have daily sets of prayer times but also pray continually (1 Thessalonians 5:17).

- Combine these in a quiet time with the Lord morning and evening.

- Belong to a Bible-believing Christian church. That is, have fellowship with other Christians and be a member of a small cell group.

- Practise "spiritual breathing" of immediately confessing any known sin, receiving forgiveness and the Spirit's infilling in order to go on. Make restitution or offer an apology when others are involved.

STEP 7: *Make Jesus your model* (Romans 12:1-3). Obedience to and imitation of Christ becomes the Christian's rule of life. You will always walk in integrity if you ask, "What would Jesus have me do?"

STEP 8: *Be aware of your "enemies."* Watch out for those things that threaten your integrity, such as sexual immorality, bribery, selfishness, or abuse of power, and develop strategies to defeat them. Everyone should know his areas of weakness. Live in the real world but don't become corrupted by it. We are to be as wise as serpents and as innocent as doves.

> WATCH OUT FOR THOSE THINGS THAT THREATEN YOUR INTEGRITY, SUCH AS SEXUAL IMMORALITY, BRIBERY, SELFISHNESS, OR ABUSE OF POWER, AND DEVELOP STRATEGIES TO DEFEAT THEM.

If there is a single factor that makes a leader dysfunctional and ineffective, in the light of the privileges, costs, and temptations of leadership, it is the lack of integrity. If you are to lead yourself, your wife, family, and followers, you must rank integrity high.

THE IMPORTANCE OF INTEGRITY

Why stress integrity? Let me conclude with biblical reasons why integrity is the foundation of Christian leadership:

- Integrity guides and preserves life (Proverbs 11:3 and Psalm 25:21) and gives confidence (1 Samuel 12:1-5).

- It enables blessings to flow to future generations (Proverbs 20:7).

- It authenticates testimony. We are ambassadors of Christ!.

- It is required of leaders by followers and gives a model for them to follow (2 Corinthians 3:18).

- It's what families, organisations, communities, and nations need most from their leaders. "Righteousness exalts a nation" (Proverbs 14:34).

- "Slightly soiled, greatly reduced." Without integrity, the value of your leadership diminishes.

- Remember that man looks at the outward appearance but God looks at the heart (1 Samuel 16:7). To God, integrity is everything.

Strive to be a person of integrity but don't be paranoid about it, because if you are, legalism or self-righteousness may undermine the very integrity you seek. Remember that the righteous may fall seven times and yet rise again! (Proverbs 24:16).

QUESTIONS:

1. What things tempt you most to compromise your integrity?

2. How can a father's lack of integrity create problems for his children?

3. How can having a strong Christian mentor help you keep on the path of integrity and righteousness?

COME, LET'S CHANGE
THE WORLD —
ONE FAMILY AT A TIME

I have not written this book as an expert family leader. I have done it as a husband and father who strives to provide leadership to his wife and four children. In fact, it was with great trepidation that I accepted the invitation in 2002 to address a retreat on effective male leadership. It was my first. But the result of the retreat paid off.

In the preceding chapters, I have sought to share some insights, drawn from the Bible and experience, regarding how, as men, we can organize our personal lives as leaders. The chapters on leading and managing oneself and effective time management were aimed at that. Leading your family is, however, a practical job that must take place in the home. To that end, I looked at the Christian home as a place of worship, a place of love, and a place where we learn living, good work ethics, and respect for authority. Within that context, the man as the head of the family is to lead his wife and children with integrity, both as a spiritual calling and as a social obligation.

I believe that the great tragedy of our day is that the family is not being given adequate attention. The school, the community, the government, even the social worker seem to assume the role of the father. As much as all these institutions have roles to play in modern society, there is no substitute for a Christian home and family leadership. Effective male leadership of the family is therefore one of the crying needs of our day.

I want to invite Christian husbands and fathers to come with me to help change our world one family at a time. It is as challenging as it is rewarding. We are called to be servant leaders of our homes for God's glory and the welfare of those we are privileged to lead and who call us husband and father!

NOTES

CHAPTER ONE

1. From a brochure by Promise Keepers. P.O. Box 11798 Denver, CO 80211-0798
2. Chinua Achebe, *Things Fall Apart* (UK: Anchor Books, 1958).
3. Myles Munroe, *Becoming a Leader: Everyone Can Do It* (Bakersfield, Calif.: Pneuma Life Publishing, 1999).

CHAPTER TWO

1. J. Oswald Sanders, *Spiritual Leadership* (Chicago: Moody Bible Institute, 1980), p. 11.
2. J. Robert Clinton, *The Making of a Leader* (Colorado Springs, Colo.: NavPress, 1998).
3. Ibid.
4. From a speech by Dr. John Hunter delivered in Accra, Ghana, in 1974.

CHAPTER THREE

1. Stephen Covey, A. R. Merrill, and R. R. Merrill, *First Things First* (London: Simon & Schuster, 1999).
2. Based on Bruce Bickel and Stan Jantz, *God Is in the Small Stuff* (New York: Promise Publishers, 1998).
3. Covey et al., *First Things First*.

CHAPTER FOUR

1. From Stephen Adei, *Twelve Keys to Financial Success* (Geneva, Switzerland: Oasis International Limited, 2001).

2. From a monograph by Stephen Adei, "Balancing the Personal, Relational, and Public Life of the Parliamentarian" (Accra: GIMPA, 2002).

CHAPTER FIVE

1. Stephen Covey, A. R. Merrill, and R. R. Merrill, *First Things First* (London: Simon & Schuster, 1999).

CHAPTER NINE

1. This chapter reproduces material from the booklet *How to Raise Good Kids in a Bad World,* by Stephen and Georgina Adei (Accra: Institute of Family and Marriage Enrichment, 2000).

CHAPTER TEN

1. James M. Kouzes and Barry Z. Posner, *Encouraging the Heart: A Leader's Guide to Rewarding and Recognizing Others* (San Francisco: Jossey-Bass Publishers, 2003).
2. This quote and the following paragraphs in this section are based in part on notes on integrity in the *Leadership Bible.* (Nashville: Thomas Nelson Publishing, 2003), p. 320.
3. James M. Kouzes, Barry Z. Posner, and Tom Peters, *Credibility: How Leaders Gain and Lose It, Why People Demand It* (New York: Jossey-Bass Publishers, 2003).
4. Stephen Covey, *Principle-Centred Leadership* (London: Simon & Schuster, 1999).

REFERENCES

BOOKS BY STEPHEN ADEI

Balancing Personal, Relational and Public Life of the Parliamentarian. Monograph. Accra: GIMPA, 2003.

The Joy of Human Love: Love, Friendship and Romance in Christian Marriage. Accra: African Christian Press, 1999.

The Secret of a Happy Marriage: Communication. 1st ed. Accra: African Christian Press, 1991.

Twelve Keys to Financial Success: A Guide to Financial Independence. Geneva: Oasis International Limited, 2001.

BOOKS BY STEPHEN AND GEORGINA ADEI

The Challenge of Parenting: Principles and Practices of Raising Children. Accra: African Christian Press, 1991.

How to Raise Good Kids in a Bad World. Accra: GIMPA, 2002.

Marriage and Family Life Mission. Counseling Manual. Kehe: Family Life Mission, 1986.

Pathway to Intimate Christian Marriage. Institute of Family and Marriage Enrichment. Accra: GIMPA, 2002.

Seven Keys to Abundant Living with No Regrets. 1st ed. Accra: African Christian Press, 1997.

God's Master Plan for Christian Marriage. Forthcoming.

ADDITIONAL RESOURCES

Achebe, Chinua. *Things Fall Apart.* New York: Anchor Books, 1958.

Bickel, Bruce and Stan Jantz. *God Is in the Small Stuff: And It All Matters.* New York: Promise Publishers, 1998.

Covey, Stephen. *Principle-Centred Leadership.* London: Simon & Schuster, 1999.

Covey, Stephen. *The Seven Habits of Highly Effective People: Powerful Lessons in Personal Change.* London: Simon & Schuster, 1990.

Covey, Stephen, A. Roger Merrill, and R. Rebecca Merrill. *First Things First: Coping with the Ever Increasing Demands of the Workplace.* London: Simon & Schuster, 1999.

Crabb, Lawrence J. Jr. *The Marriage Builder.* Grand Rapids, Mich.: Zondervan Publishing House, 1982.

Dobson, James C. *Dare to Discipline.* Wheaton, Ill.: Tyndale House Publishers, 1987.

Ekuta, Jethro. *Marriage as God Intended It to Be.* Ozark; Alabama: ACW Press, 2001.

Gray, John. *Men Are from Mars, Women Are from Venus: A Practical Guide for Improving Communication and Getting What You Want in Your Relationships.* New York: HarperCollins, 1993.

Greenleaf, R. K. *Servant Leadership*. New York: Paulist Press, 1997.

Harley, W. F. Jr. *His Needs, Her Needs: Building an Affair-Proof Marriage*. Grand Rapids: Mich.: Revell, 2001.

Hill, Polly. *The Migrant Cocoa Farmers of Southern Ghana: A Study in Rural Capitalism*. (Classics in African Anthropology Series). 2nd ed. London: Lit. Verleg, 1999.

Jones, E. Stanley. *Abundant Living*. Reprinted ed. London: Abingdon Press, 1990.

Kotter, J. P. *Leading Change: Why Transformation Efforts Fail*. Harvard Business Review Vol. 73., No. 2:59-67, 1995.

Kotter, J. P. *What Leaders Really Do*. Boston: Harvard Business School Press, 1999.

Kouzes, James M. and Barry Z. Posner. *Encouraging the Heart: A Leader's Guide to Rewarding and Recognizing Others*. 1st ed. San Francisco: Jossey-Bass Publishers, 2003.

Kouzes, James M., Barry Z. Posner, and Tom Peters. *Credibility: How Leaders Gain and Lose It, Why People Demand It*. New York: Jossey-Bass Publishers; San Francisco: Simon & Schuster, 1995.

Maxwell, John C. *Developing the Leader Within You*. 2nd ed. Nashville, Tenn.: Thomas Nelson Publishers, 2000.

Maxwell, John C. *Developing the Leaders Around You: How to Help Others Reach Their Full Potential*. Abridged ed. Nashville, Tenn.: Thomas Nelson Publishers, 2003.

Maxwell, John C. *The 21 Irrefutable Laws of Leadership: Follow Them and People Will Follow You*. Nashville, Tenn.: Thomas Nelson Publishers, 1998.

Meyer, Paul J., and Randy Slechta. *The 5 Pillars of Leadership: How to Bridge the Leadership Gap.* Tulsa: Okla.: Insight Publishing Group, 2002.

Munroe, Myles. *Becoming a Leader: Everyone Can Do It.* Bakersfield, Calif.: Pneuma Life Publishing, 1999.

Sanders, J. Oswald. *Spiritual Leadership: Principles of Excellence for Every Believer.* Revised ed. Chicago: Moody Publishers, 1994.

Schoolland, Marian M., with illustrations by Paul Stoub. *Leading Little Ones to God: A Child's Book of Bible Teachings.* Grand Rapids, Mich.: William Eerdmans Publishing, 1995.

Swindoll, Charles R. *Hand Me Another Brick.* Nashville, Tenn.: Thomas Nelson Publishing, 1998.

Taylor, Kenneth N. *Stories for the Children's Hour.* Chicago: Moody Press, 1968.

FOCUS ON THE FAMILY

WELCOME TO THE FAMILY!

Whether you received this book as a gift, borrowed it from a friend, or purchased it yourself, we're glad you read it. It's just one of the many helpful, insightful and encouraging resources produced by Focus on the Family.

In fact, that's what Focus on the Family is all about-providing inspiration, information and biblically based advice to people in all stages of life.

It began in 1977 with the vision of one man, Dr. James Dobson, a licensed psychologist and author of 16 best-selling books on marriage, parenting, and family. Alarmed by the societal, political, and economic pressures that were threatening the existence of the American family, Dr. Dobson founded Focus on the Family with one employee—an assistant—and a once-a-week radio broadcast, aired on only 36 stations.

Now an international organization, Focus on the Family is dedicated to preserving Judeo-Christian values and strengthening and encouraging families through the life-changing message of Jesus Christ. Focus ministries reach families worldwide through 10 separate radio broadcasts, two television news features, 13 publications, 18 Web sites, and a steady series of books and award-winning films and videos for people of all ages and interests.

Visit our Web site—www.family.org—to learn more about Focus on the Family or to find out if there is an associate office in your country.

We'd love to hear from you!

For further information about the author, please contact:

Institute of Family and Marriage Enrichment
P.O. Box S413
Mile Seven
Accra, Ghana

Or, via e-mail at: adeistephen@yahoo.uk.co